PILATES
FOR HORSES

*A Mind-Body Conditioning Program
for Strength, Mobility, and Performance*

Laura Reiman, MS, PMA-CPT

Trafalgar Square
North Pomfret, Vermont

First published in 2021 by
Trafalgar Square Books
North Pomfret, Vermont 05053

Disclaimer of Liability
The author and publisher shall have neither liability nor responsibility to any person or entity with respect to any loss or damage caused or alleged to be caused directly or indirectly by the information contained in this book. While the book is as accurate as the author can make it, there may be errors, omissions, and inaccuracies.

This book is meant to be an educational resource only. It is always best to consult a professional for equine training and medical care.

Trafalgar Square Books encourages the use of approved safety helmets in all equestrian sports and activities.

Library of Congress Cataloging-in-Publication Data
Names: Reiman, Laura, author.
Title: Pilates for horses : a mind-body conditioning program for strength, mobility, and performance / Laura Reiman, MS, PMA-CPT.
Description: North Pomfret, Vermont : Trafalgar Square Books, 2021. | Includes index. | Summary: "This highly illustrated how-to manual provides a clear guide to new ways of thinking about how to prevent injury in the horse, and when injuries do happen, to help the horse's body recover in a mindful and safe way. As a Pilates teacher for humans, horse-woman and eventer Laura Reiman has seen first-hand how consistent, quality exercise can ward off strain and injury, as well as heal. When her young horse was diagnosed with extreme back pain and a neurological disease, she turned to her knowledge of Pilates-the method she'd used to ease back pain in human clients for years-for help. She began to find ways to "bridge the gap" between the horse's mind and body to help increase his body awareness and core engagement"-- Provided by publisher.
Identifiers: LCCN 2020045505 (print) | LCCN 2020045506 (ebook) | ISBN 9781570769788 (paperback) | ISBN 9781646010905 (epub)
Subjects: LCSH: Equine sports medicine. | Pilates method. | Horses--Health.
Classification: LCC SF956 .R45 2021 (print) | LCC SF956 (ebook) | DDC 636.108955--dc23
LC record available at https://lccn.loc.gov/2020045505
LC ebook record available at https://lccn.loc.gov/2020045506

All photographs by Erin Gilmore Photography except figs. I.1 A, 3.4, 3.9, 4.8 B, 4.9 A & B, 4.10 A & B, 4.11 A & B, 4.13 B, 5.3, 5.4, 6.2, 6.3, 7.2 A & B, 7.4, 8.7 A & B, 8.8 A & B, 8.9, 8.15, 9.2, 9.3 C, 9.5 and B on p. 186 by Roberta Reiman and I.1 by Christopher Boyer

Illustrations by Jurre Blom
Book design by Lauryl Eddlemon
Cover design by RM Didier
Index by Andrea M. Jones (www.jonesliteraryservices.com)
Typefaces: Fontina Sans; Gotham

Printed in China

10 9 8 7 6 5 4 3 2 1

For my mother,
who instilled a great love of horses
in me from a young age.

Contents

165

Introduction

As a Pilates teacher and studio owner, nutritionist, and certified personal trainer, I have seen firsthand how movement can heal. Consistent, quality exercise can prevent injury and when injuries do happen, these same exercises can be modified to help the body slowly and carefully recover in a mindful and safe way.

When my five-year-old, off-the-track Thoroughbred named Mark, was diagnosed with extreme back pain and, eventually, a neurological disease called EPM, or Equine Protozoal Myeloencephalitis, I turned to Pilates—a method I'd used to help ease back pain and strengthen clients for years—for help. I went to work bridging the gap between Mark's mind and body, using the same resistance bands and stability pads I had in my studio to help increase body awareness and core engagement for my horse. I had to consult many different books as well as multiple vets and equine therapists to find the stretches, groundwork, and under-saddle work that my horse needed. I used my knowledge of the human body and how it works to tailor each exercise for my horse and my abilities as an amateur rider.

I.1 I bought my event horse Bold Mark just a few months after he retired from racing. Less than two months later, he started showing odd signs of discomfort, eventually leading to a diagnosis of EPM. I patiently and progressively rehabbed Mark back to health using one of the tools I know best—Pilates.

CHECK WITH YOUR VET

It's important to have veterinarian approval before beginning any work after an injury or when you suspect your horse may have an underlying, undiagnosed injury. Use these exercises at your own risk and always err on the side of caution when trying new things. Thoughtful and correct rehabilitation takes time and patience. Good luck!

I.2 A & B Pilates often incorporates tools such as resistance bands to help stretch and strengthen muscles. Many of these same tools can be used for your horse. Not only do resistance bands increase proprioception—that is, more awareness of where and what the limbs are doing—but they also gently increase the weight your horse must push against to propel forward, aiding in the strengthening of the hind end.

This book is meant to be a guide for everyone—amateur owners and pro-fessionals alike, from all disciplines. *Pilates for Horses* is for all people looking to build and maintain a solid foundation of strength and comfort for their horse, even if they are lacking professional dressage capabilities. As riders, we often warm up and stretch our bodies for exercise but forget our horses need that same time and attention as well—this book shows you where to start.

These exercises can be taken in parts or as a whole and can be seam-lessly incorporated into an existing training program as a preventive tool to increase strength, balance, mobility, and stability, or as the framework for a new program to help ease a horse back into work following an injury or time off.

PART ONE

Fundamentals

Before learning the *Pilates for Horses* exercises, it's a good idea to have a basic understanding of what Pilates is, what your horse's needs are, and the "why" behind what you're doing. Having a general knowledge of equine anatomy and muscle function is the first step in creating a successful program for you and your horse.

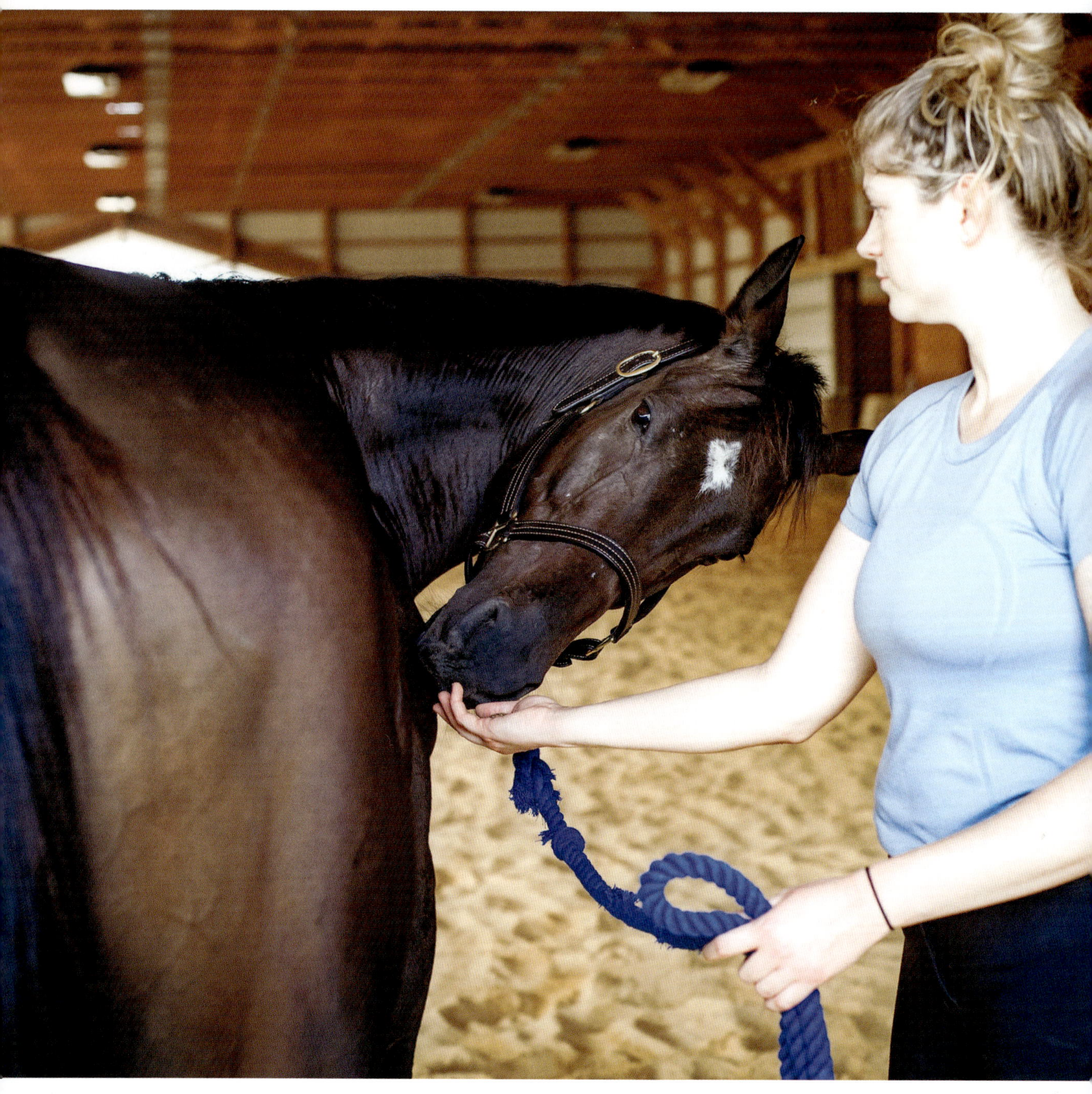

Getting to Know Pilates

What Is Pilates?

Pilates is a mind-body conditioning method that trains the whole body for quality, efficient movement. This exercise modality emphasizes flexibility, strength, control, and balance through progressive and safe movement.

Pilates was created by a man named Joseph Pilates who went from being a sickly child with rickets, asthma, and rheumatic fever to a being a model for anatomy charts as well as a fitness pioneer. He was born in Germany in 1883 and spent his early years studying an array of Eastern and Western exercises and philosophies, borrowing ideas from gymnastics, bodybuilding, boxing, fencing, yoga, and other forms of movement to improve his own health and well-being.

During World War I, Pilates was interned in a camp on the Isle of Man where he was tasked with rehabilitating the sick and disabled within the camp. Continuing his exploration of acquiring a healthy body, Pilates helped his "patients" get better faster and strengthen both their body and their immune system. By the time he came to America in the early 1920s, he had devised his own movement method named "Contrology." Contrology prioritized nourishing the body as a whole and was considered a lifestyle just as much as an

1.1 Horses, like humans, are athletes. Their muscles must be stretched as well as strengthened for optimum health. Here you can see one such stretch: Nose to Girth (p. 61).

exercise program. After his death in 1967, Contrology became known simply as Pilates.

While some people continue to practice Pilates just as it was created by the man himself, other practitioners have chosen a more contemporary approach, using the exercises and ideas Joseph Pilates extolled as a framework and building upon it using new research and knowledge about the body and what it needs today. It is this contemporary approach that lends itself so well to the equine body.

Most importantly, Pilates is beneficial for *every* body and *every* mind. And, while there is no replacement for professional training, these exercises can be done by all equestrians to help support their horses.

This book is not about having a perfect frame or being able to tell if your horse is the ideal anatomical specimen. It's about having tools to help support your horse's health in a safe and effective way. These tools will help you stretch and strengthen your horse's muscles without the constant supervision of specialists and trainers, and will empower amateurs and professionals alike to help their horse find optimal health and movement.

What Is Pilates for Horses?

Pilates for Horses takes the principles of Pilates and the benefits we have seen humans gain from the method, and applies it to our equine partners. Research and experience has shown that much of what benefits humans in the prevention and rehabilitation of injuries can be applied to horses with similar beneficial outcomes.

Principles of Pilates Applied to Horses

Control, center, concentration, precision, breath, and *flow* are the original principles of Pilates. *Awareness, balance, efficiency, alignment, coordination, stamina, lengthening,* and *harmony* can also be considered key components of the method. All of these principles relate to how our horses should optimally move.

Control: This concept is defined as regulating a given action with few or minor errors. This means activating the correct muscles at the correct time with exacting balance, coordination, consistency, and refinement. This is essential for having quality gaits and transitions, and requires acute awareness of the body and limbs for both horse and rider.

Center: The center of the body is a single point from which the rest of the body is equally distributed and balanced. For the equine, this principle best applies to the *core*, which acts as a bridge between the front and hind end, and through which energy must flow freely. It is essential to have a strong and stable center for the rest of the body to move effectively.

Concentration: Concentration requires channeling your horse's energy and focus onto a single task or exercise. Your horse must have concentration in order to correctly place his feet over poles, find a good distance when jumping, and even during flatwork when asked for transitions both within and between gaits, and in lateral movement. Concentration means being attentive without tension.

Precision: Precision means being specific in the execution of an exercise. It is through exacting movement that you can isolate smaller muscles and optimize strength benefits from each exercise. This is an important part of moving efficiently and effectively instead of simply relying on pure strength to get something done. Quality is key: it is important that your horse responds to your aid when you apply it, and not 10 strides later. Think of your upward transition to canter. You want him to engage his hindquarters and spring into the canter, not run into it from a quick trot.

Breath: Have you ever noticed how long it takes your horse to snort or loudly exhale when you're riding? Does your horse hold his breath during work and release during rest? Breathing patterns are a good indication of stress and tension, and horses are much less likely to build healthy muscles when working tense. Pay attention to your horse's breath and make changes to your riding as necessary. This also applies to making sure the abdominals and muscles surrounding the rib cage and underside of the body, or extensor chain, are supple so there isn't excessive tightness through the ribs, allowing for full and deep breathing. The more oxygen your horse takes in, the healthier the heart and lungs will be.

Flow: A well-balanced horse should look like he is flowing—or dancing—from one transition to another. It is often said that the horse's body is like a machine of interconnected pulleys and levers, and one movement affects the entire body. Not only must you have flow through the body without "sticky" bits of muscling or knots within the fascia, you must have flow through the gaits and between your aids and the movement. Flow means smooth, graceful, functional movement.

Awareness: Horses are very good at creating compensatory movement patterns after dealing with an injury or gait abnormality. Just like people, habits can become familiar and difficult to break. An important step in rebalancing the body is to make your horse aware of his own abilities and compensations, and support the formation of new, proper movement. Correct cues or aids are essential in reprogramming your horse's awareness of what he should be doing and how, and props such as stability pads and resistance bands can help challenge the nervous system and build awareness for your horse.

Balance: Most horses have asymmetries somewhere in their body, which makes it that much harder—and inefficient—to find balance. It is important to strengthen muscles evenly, not just on both sides of the horse, but also front and back and top to bottom. When the shoulders become too strong, the horse can fall to the forehand, which tips his balance forward. When the hind becomes too strong without flexibility, range of motion can be impeded. When a horse favors one side, he may end up letting that side do all the work so it continues to stay dominant and tight. The body must be strengthened as a whole to maintain balance.

Alignment: As with balance, regardless of your horse's anatomy, you should strive for symmetrical muscles and straight, even movement on both the right and left side. Can you move down the centerline with all your horse's body parts from poll to tail in alignment, no shoulder or hip rotated or popped out? Do your horse's back feet track directly in line with the front feet? Does your horse drift off a straight line? Proper strengthening and stretching is essential for maintaining correct alignment.

Efficiency: Quality work with as little effort as possible is the ultimate goal in Pilates and, in my opinion, in riding. For example, fit event horses and foxhunters are able to gallop miles of cross-country jumps because the conditioning work done in advance has created efficient muscles, and therefore, less energy is expended than if an underconditioned horse attempts the same work. I once complained to my trainer that I was exhausted after a 30-minute ride. He explained that I was not using my body efficiently or effectively, so I was overriding and overworking my muscles. Professionals are often able to ride multiple horses a day without fatigue because they have learned to use their body efficiently, getting more from the horse with less effort and strength expended. If a horse can efficiently use his body, he will exert less effort and be less fatigued after working.

Coordination: Coordination is the ability to move two or more body parts in a controlled and balanced way. This is obtained through both core strength and stability work, as well as repetition and proprioception exercises, such as ground poles, cavalletti, gymnastics, and hill work. These mind-body exercises force your horse to figure out how to place his feet in order to continue moving forward, which challenges the nervous system and ultimately increases your horse's confidence in where his body and limbs are in space.

Stamina: Stamina is the ability to maintain quality movement for a sustained amount of time, and must be built up slowly and thoughtfully. As your horse's stamina increases, he may also seem more eager to work. Horses can build stamina through repetition of exercises, cardio conditioning days and interval training, and through progressive strengthening of the muscles.

Lengthening: Lengthening is essential for your horse in several different ways. Not only must muscles be stretched and lengthened as they are strengthened in order to maintain flexibility and full range of motion, but it also refers to the elongation of the stride. Lengthening the gait requires a harnessing of energy and should increase the "springiness" and power of your horse's movement.

Harmony: Horse and rider must work together to achieve the best quality movement. Your horse should respond quickly and smoothly to your aids without fighting or resisting. With balance often comes harmony.

These principles make up the foundation of Pilates and can be used as a guide when setting goals or deciding which exercises your horse needs each day. For instance, if you want to work on stamina, high intensity interval training (HIIT, see p. 160), is a great exercise to include in your program. To address coordination, gymnastics can be included in your training (see p. 157). Ride each session with your goals and the Pilates principles in mind.

What Is Strength?

Strength is the maximum force a muscle can apply in one contraction. For instance, think of the force needed from your horse's hind end to press away from the ground and launch more than 1,000 pounds over a jump. The stronger the muscle, the greater force it can apply. The stronger the hind end, the higher the horse can jump successfully.

When a muscle contracts with progressively more difficult resistance or force against it, it will increase in size. This is called *hypertrophy*. Think of how weight lifters build muscles and strength by slowly adding more weight to their lifts. **Muscles need to be overloaded by 75 percent of maximum potential resistance just twice a week for hypertrophy or strength gains to occur.** That means a weight lifter who continuously lifts at an easy level (below 75 percent maximum effort) won't get stronger. This is often referred to as a "plateau" and can be confusing—you might ask yourself, why are we putting in the work and not getting any better? But, the resistance may not be great enough. This also means that trotting aimlessly around the arena won't necessarily make your horse stronger because you need continuous, progressive challenges for his muscles.

When there are no contractions, muscles can decrease in size or *atrophy*. When my horse was sick with EPM and could not activate his right hind gluteal, the muscle atrophied and the right side of his hind end looked like it had deflated. As he came back into work, the muscles slowly began to fill out again.

As muscles grow stronger, however, they shorten. This is why body builders often cannot touch their toes. In order to prevent losing range of motion, stretching and flexibility training must go hand in hand with strength training.

Basic Muscle Function

A contraction refers to the creation of tension within a muscle. There are two types of muscle contraction, *isometric* and *isotonic*.

An *isometric* contraction is a static or holding position where muscle force is equal to resistance force. In this contraction, there is no change in the length of the muscle or the angle of the joint. This is typically what stabilizer muscles are used for. As an example, the *abdominals* will use an isometric contraction to stabilize the torso during suspension.

An *isotonic* contraction is contraction of the muscle through movement or range of motion, against resistance. There are two types of *isotonic* contraction, *concentric* and *eccentric*:

- *Concentric* contraction is a shortening of the muscle. The angle of the joint will decrease and there will be a muscular force higher than the force of resistance. Think of this as propulsion. For example, the stifle uses concentric contraction during takeoff when jumping or when traveling up a hill.

- *Eccentric* contraction is a lengthening of the muscle during contraction. The angle of the joint will increase and the muscle force is less than the resistance. Think of this as the loading phase and how muscles have the ability to harness energy and then repurpose it like a spring. For example, the *supraspinatus* muscle activates in an eccentric contraction to stop the

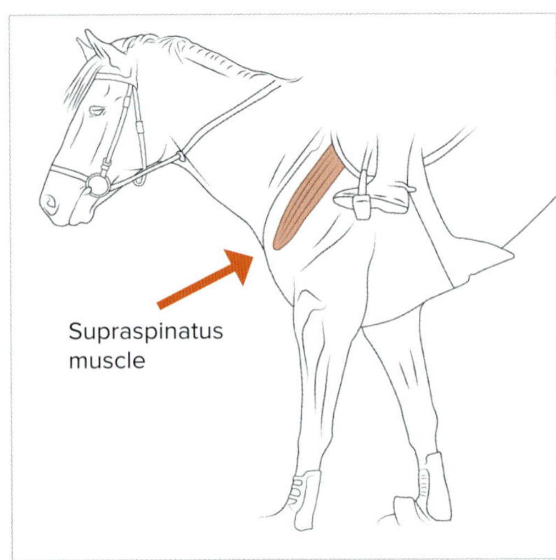

1.2 The activation of the *supraspinatus* muscle during landing is an example of an *eccentric* contraction.

shoulder joint from closing when landing from a jump (fig. 1.2).

Every movement requires two sets of muscles (fig. 1.3). One to *contract* and the other side to *lengthen and release* in order to allow the movement. Sometimes both will contract in order to *stabilize* or *balance*.

- The *agonist* is the primary mover/muscle that shortens.

- The *antagonist* is the opposite muscle that releases. For example, when the *rectus abdominus* is contracted, the *longissimus dorsi* must release. When the *gluteal* muscles release, the *obliques* must engage (see fig. 1.3).

- *Stabilizer* muscles support the rest of the body while the movement occurs. These are often the abdominal, or *core* muscles.

- *Co-contractors* are muscles that work together to perform a movement. For example, the abdominals contract with the loins to round and lift the back.

Why Is Stretching So Important?

Stretching is essential in order to improve—and even just maintain—optimal length of muscles and fascia, especially when gaining strength. Longer muscle fibers mean more elasticity and suppleness.

Stretching increases circulation and decreases pull or strain on tendons near the muscles, two important things to prevent injury. When a muscle is tight, it can pull on the connecting area where tendons meet bone, which can cause strain or inflammation. Fascia can also get "sticky" or knotted without proper stretching, which then inhibits range of motion and flow of movement.

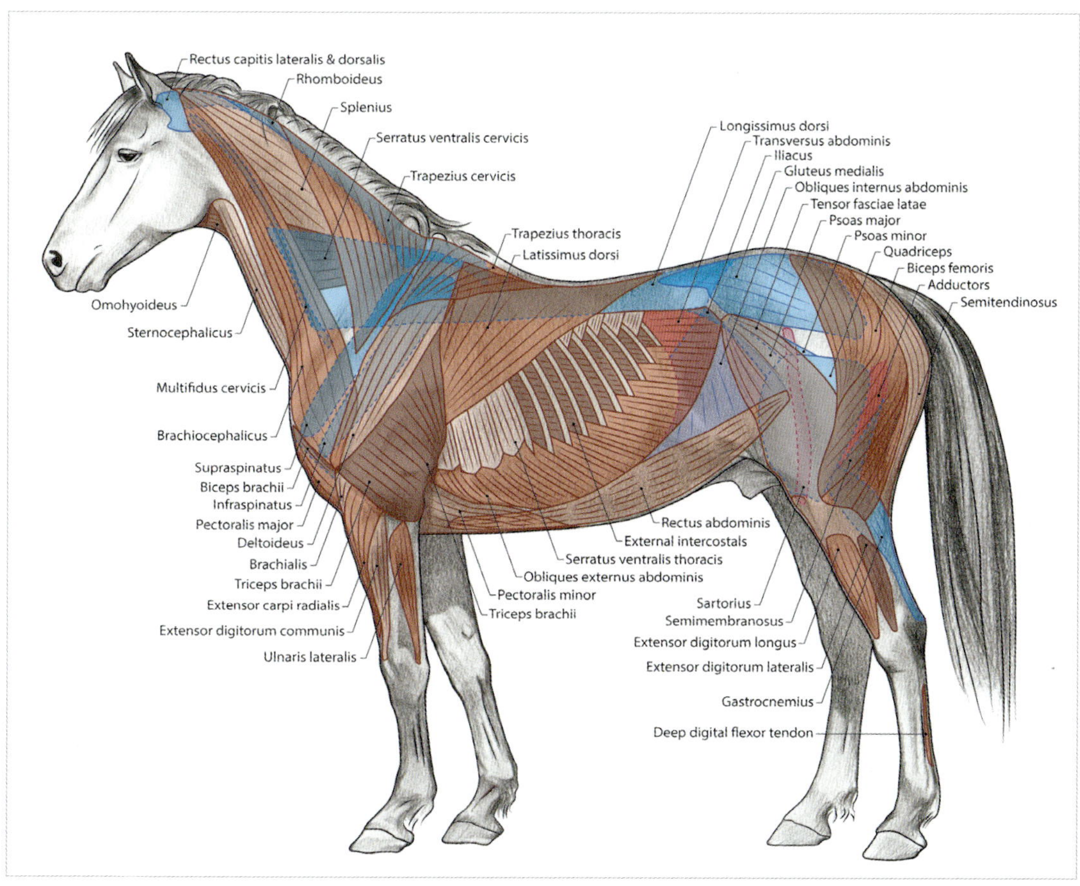

1.3 Some of the more important muscles of the horse to remember.

In the horse, stretching can:

- Improve body awareness
- Improve coordination
- Quicken reflexes
- Relax or ease tension
- Relieve muscle pain
- Improve circulation
- Promote elasticity of soft tissue
- Prevent muscle strain
- Increase mobility and flexibility

There are two types of stretching: *static* and *dynamic. Dynamic* stretches are mobilizing, active movements that stretch the body through a full range of motion. *Static* stretches are held at the end-range of current muscle flexibility without movement, allowing the muscle to relax and release into a stretch. Both are beneficial.

Flexibility is considered the range of motion of a joint. This is slightly reliant on genetics and the shape of the joint itself, but flexibility can also be manipulated by the elasticity of connective tissue, strength of opposing muscles, and the neurological coordination of related muscles.

A good Pilates program incorporates a balanced amount of strength and stretching, which can also be thought of as *stability* and *mobility* work.

Stability vs. Mobility

Stability is the capacity to maintain posture and control, supporting the body so that other muscles or joints can safely and properly mobilize. Stability muscles are typically closer to the joint and are most often slow-twitch/aerobic muscles. *Slow-twitch* muscle fibers take longer to engage but are more energy efficient and suited for lower intensity, endurance-demanding work than *fast-twitch muscles*, which are used for stronger, shorter bursts of action like sprinting or spooking (fig. 1.4).

Mobility is the speed, power, and motor function of movement. The more mobile the spine, the more range of motion the limbs typically have. When a horse is too tight, he won't have the flow and mobility needed to move efficiently.

Just as with humans, poor ratio of stability and mobility as well as gait irregularities can leave some muscles underutilized or completely unable to fire. This becomes a cycle of stronger muscles taking over while weaker muscles become even less engaged. *Core* muscles in particular can be difficult to isolate.

SLOW-TWITCH MUSCLE FIBERS	FAST-TWITCH MUSCLE FIBERS
Low, slow force	Big, quick force
Fatigues slowly	Fatigues quickly
Long-term contraction	Short-term contraction
Endurance activity	Power activity
Tends to be smaller muscles	Tends to be bigger muscles
Endurance, stability, posture	Racing, jumping, agility
Typically used during aerobic exercise or lower intensity work with adequate fuel and oxygen present	Typically used during anaerobic exercise or higher intensity work in non-oxygen conditions that leads to fatigue

1.4

Why Is the Core So Important?

Core muscles are not only a bridge connecting the scapula and pelvis (front and hind end), they create suspension/elevation, allow for flexion and round-ness, and are essential for straightness and balance.

It is important that the core not only be strong, but supple. A supple core is one that can bend comfortably, move energy efficiently through the body, and create harmonious turns and smooth transitions. A weak core can lead to a hard, stiff neck and mouth, an inverted back, and a horse falling on the forehand instead of pushing from behind.

While we generally think of the core as the muscles that run along the lower chain of the body, the upper chain—also known as the *topline*—is just as important.

What Is the Topline?

The *topline* is considered the muscles that run along the top of the horse's body from the poll to the hamstrings, propelling the horse forward and help-ing him to cover more ground. These muscles are also known as the *extensor muscle chain* and must be both strong and supple (fig. 1.5). The shape of the topline comes from the *nuchal ligament*, the muscles in the neck, and the *thoracic* and *lumbar spinous processes*.

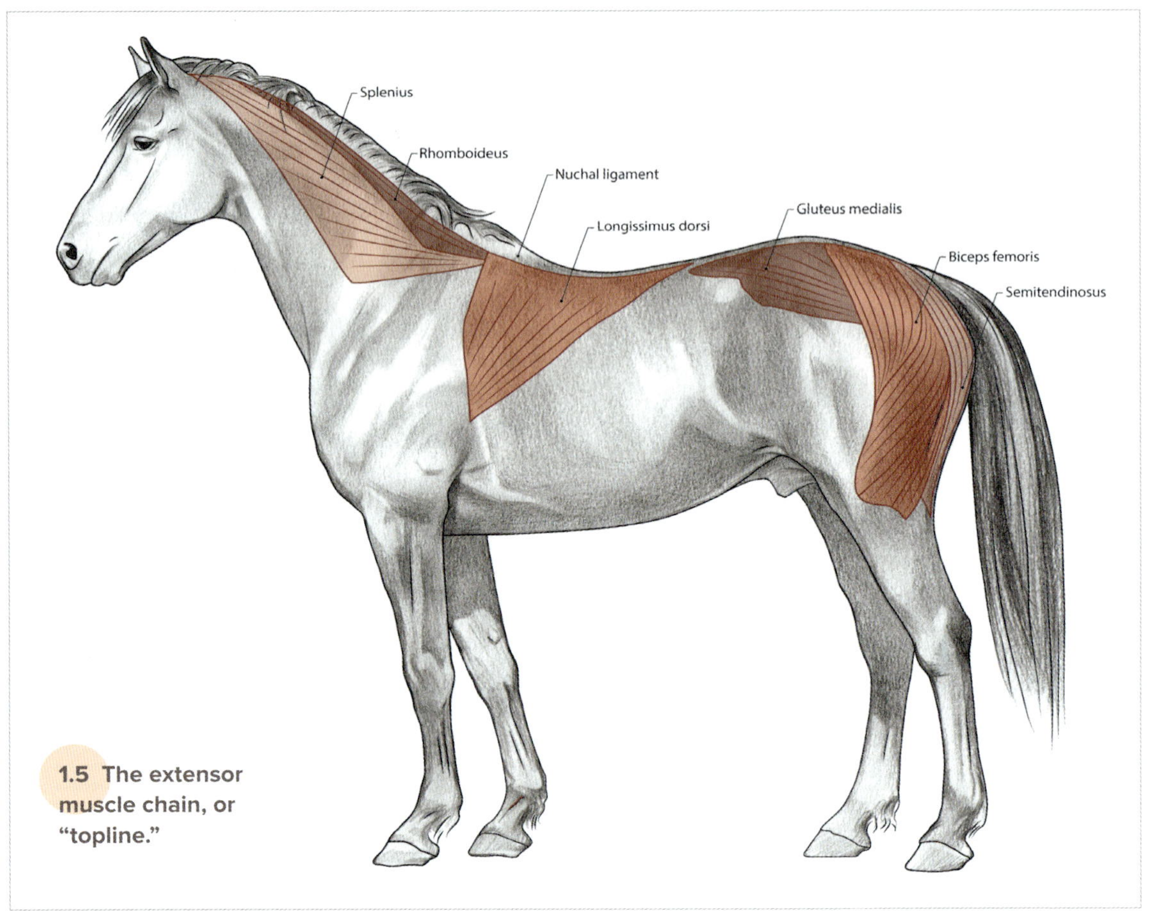

1.5 The extensor muscle chain, or "topline."

The *extensor chain* works in conjunction with the *flexor chain* (core). This goes from the tongue down the lower neck and chest and along the bottom of the horse, including the deep abdominal muscles (figs. 1.6 and 1.7). These muscles flex or round the spine and elevate the torso between the front limbs.

- If the extensor chain is strengthened without the flexor chain also strengthening, the horse can get heavy on the forehand and rush or brace against the bit and get stiff.

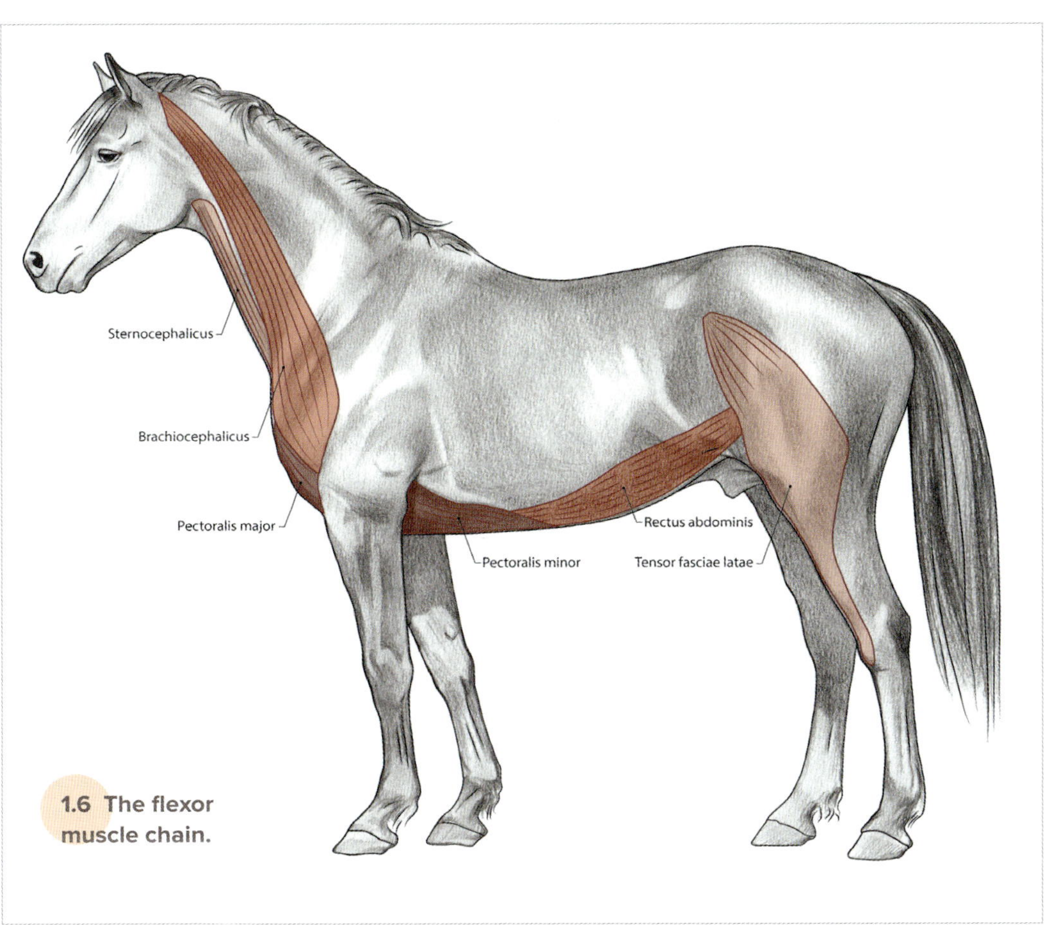

1.6 The flexor muscle chain.

MAIN EXTENSOR CHAIN MUSCLES	MAIN FLEXOR CHAIN MUSCLES
<ul><li>Hamstring group – Semitendinosus – Bicep femoris – Gluteals</li><li>Longissimus dorsi</li><li>Rhomboids</li><li>Splenius</li></ul>	<ul><li>Rectus abdominus</li><li>Pectorals</li><li>Brachiocephalicus</li><li>Sternocephalicus</li><li>Tensor fasciae latae</li></ul>

1.7

- When the horse is too strong in the extensor chain muscles (topline), there may be excess tension in the back and forward pushing muscles. This can make muscles of the flexor chain harder to recruit.

- When the core isn't strong enough and the torso hangs, there will be excess strain on the shoulders and back. The two sides must work together in harmony.

Just as the topline and flexor chain must work harmoniously, the mind must be trained to work in union with the body.

Proprioception and the Mind-Body Connection

Human and equine bodies alike are covered in sensory neurons that constantly pick up stimulus and send it to the central nervous system. These nerves pick up environmental signals as well as internal information like strain or compression that is then processed by the brain and affects reflexes, balance, coordination, and movement patterns.

Proprioception is responsible for your horse knowing where his limbs are in relation to each other, to the ground, and to the environment. Your horse's brain must not only process where he is within his environment, but also associate rider aids to the correct movements. You must always be aware of your aids, as your horse is learning every time you interact with him. Stay consistent in order to help educate your horse's mind as it connects to the body.

Creating a Program for Your Horse

Every horse is different, just as every human body is different. They all have individual needs and react uniquely to training both mentally and physically. There is no substitute for a good trainer, knowledgeable vet, and a certified body worker when appropriate, but all riders should have a general knowledge of equine anatomy and the tools to help their horse be successful on a day-to-day basis.

A good program with proper schooling will train both the body and the brain to support a balanced and willing equine partner. The goal should always be progressive, building at a slow pace that allows time for soft tissue to catch up to your horse's cardiovascular fitness and abilities. The horse's body, much like our own, adapts to mild strain by increasing bone density. Therefore, you should plan to gradually increase demand so the body can adapt without injury.

Muscles can take up to six months to reach peak fitness, but connective tissue and ligaments can take one to two years to fully strengthen after starting a new program. Have patience and set goals that can evolve over time, increasing the difficulty of just one element of your program at a time, be it frequency, intensity, or duration. Allow 10 to 14 days after beginning a new exercise or increasing workload before increasing the difficulty more.

Cross-training is important to keep in mind when planning your program. A good rule to follow is that a horse shouldn't perform the same type of work two days in a row. That way, minor tissue damage can repair in some muscles while others work. Diversity in training not only helps build different muscles, which can prevent stress injuries that occur from drilling the same type of work over and over, but it keeps the horse mentally engaged (fig. 1.8).

Pilates is not just a set of exercises, it's a whole-body wellness program. This means you should also take a closer look at your horse's nutrition, saddle fit, and turn-out situation as well as any alternative therapies like acupuncture or massage that are available in your region. If you're not sure what your horse's individual needs are, consult a trainer or veterinarian to point you in the right direction, and then use these exercises as a guide to get there.

CROSS-TRAINING GOAL	
Discipline specific flatwork	2x per week
Conditioning/ cardio rides	1x per week
Hacking/trail ride "brain breaks"	1x per week
Jumping/cavalletti	2x per week

1.8

You can also refer to the "Pyramid of Training" to get an idea of where you are and what you need to work on as your horse progresses (fig. 1.9). Even though this chart is a dressage training scale, it is applicable for all disciplines. Use the scale to set goals and remember that sometimes patience can be the hardest part of a training program.

It is also a good idea to take some time to get to know basic horse structure and function as well as your own horse's specific body before beginning a new program.

Basic Framework of the Horse

Bones provide both support and elasticity for the horse by absorbing and distributing impact, stress, and vibration. They are constantly being remodeled so it's important to have proper nutrition and training for bones to stay strong.

Why this matters: While bone shape is genetic, bone density can be changed through fitness work. Bones can get stronger from controlled stress placed on them.

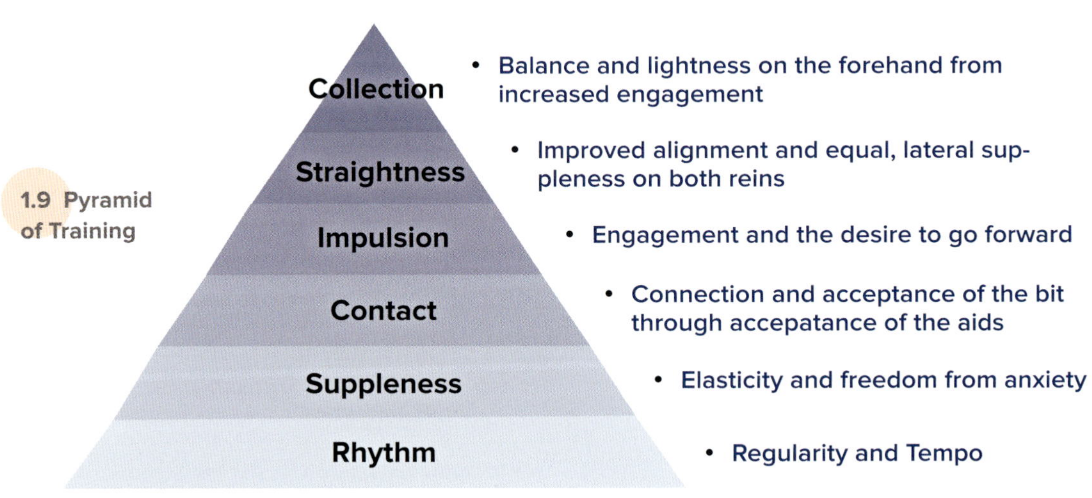

1.9 Pyramid of Training

2019 updated USDF pyramid

Joints are between two bones and act to assist or restrict movement between them.

Why this matters: Joint cartilage doesn't have blood flow. Waste is pressed out of the joint during work and nutrition is sucked back in during relaxation. When this doesn't occur, cartilage can get stiff and thick from lack of flow and weaken the joint, leading to injury.

Connective tissue refers to tendons, ligaments, cartilage, and fascia.

Why this matters: Connective tissue becomes stronger and thicker with work and is important for supporting growing muscles.

Muscles are made up of two ends and a belly. The *origin* is where the muscle attaches to the bone and is the anchor for muscle movement. The other side is the *insertion*, which is more flexible and attaches to tissues like tendons or another muscle. The most common point of stress or damage is the origin point. Muscles cannot add fibers; they simply enlarge or shrink.

Why this matters: Easy exercise cannot build muscle. In fact, prolonged and excessive tension only causes fatigue. There must be progressive resistance/overload at around 75 percent of maximum tension to build proper muscling, and therefore, strength.

Ligaments help support bones and restrict joint movement when the end range of motion is reached. Ligaments hold the joints together, provide stability, and support muscle contractions.

Why this matters: When a ligament tears or overstretches, the affected joint becomes unstable and the surrounding muscles must try to take over to support it. Often you can add specific exercises to directly target these surrounding muscles to help build strength and stability. For instance, when the stifle becomes weak or unstable due to a ligament injury, you can strengthen the *quadriceps* to help support the hind end.

Tendons connect muscle to bone and act as shock absorbers to sudden force. They are also used as backup for when muscles tire. When pressure is applied such as when landing after a jump, tendons can store energy from the impact and then rebound like a spring without using more energy. Tendons also relay muscle activity to the bone.

Why this matters: Tendons and ligaments get less blood supply than muscle tissue so it's important to increase circulation here. You can progressively build strength in tendons and ligaments just like muscle and bone since it responds the same, getting stronger with work or weaker with lack of use.

Fascia is tissue that surrounds the entire body. It wraps around muscles, nerves, and organs and binds them all together. If strained or damaged, it can decrease flexibility. Poor saddle fit, strain, injury, fatigue, and repetitive stress can easily cause damage to the fascia. This not only affects the body but also the nervous system, disrupting proprioception and sensory function. When fascia gets knotted it can become inflamed, which can lead to scar tissue and decreased range of motion.

Why this matters: Continuous work on the same exercises and muscle groups can cause fascia to become "sticky" or thick, and limit range of motion and flexibility. Exercises that stimulate proprioception, like cross-training on different surfaces (p. 99), and using ground poles (p. 104) can improve the smoothness of fascia, which translates into better balance, stability, and comfort for the horse.

chapter 2

Basic Horse Anatomy

Head and Neck

The equine neck is comprised of seven vertebrae and accounts for roughly 6 percent of your horse's total body weight. The head and neck are essential for balance, which is why we often use the neck as an indicator of strength and soundness. It is not uncommon to see a severe head bob in a lame horse because he is attempting to use his head and neck to balance off a painful limb.

Alternatively, many people view neck muscles as an indicator of training. A racing horse may have a strong underside of the neck because he reaches forward and against the bit to run. A young dressage horse is often encouraged to work long and low with the neck to help stretch and strengthen the nuchal ligament, and is then progressively asked to lift the head and neck as collection and self-carriage are introduced, creating stronger muscles along the top of the neck. While not an exhaustive list, the following are a few key neck muscles and their function (fig. 2.2).

2.1 It's a good idea to take photos of your horse regularly—from the front, side, and rear—to keep track of progress and alignment.

NUCHAL LIGAMENT

One of the most important ligaments for the rider to understand is the *nuchal ligament,* which runs from the back of the horse's skull to the withers and helps round the spine and balance the body. When the horse's head drops, the nuchal ligament pulls on the spinous processes of the withers, which arches the back up and naturally releases the core. This is why the exercise **The Stretch** (p. 130) is helpful for stretching the back.

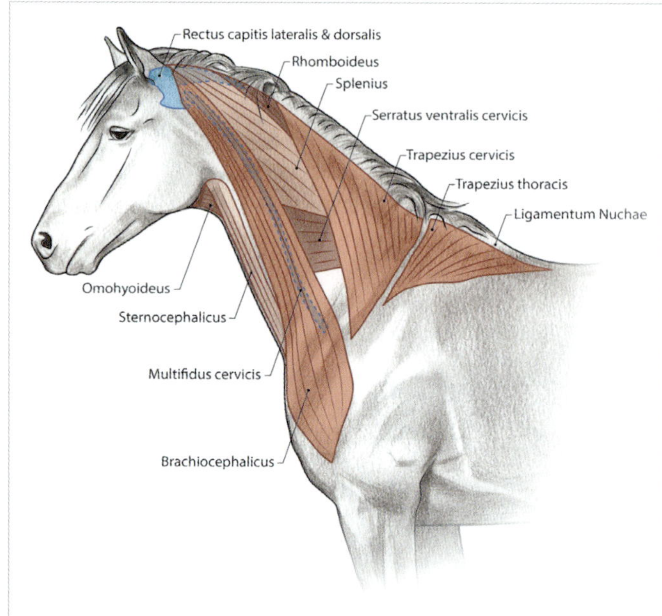

2.2 Some of the muscles of the horse's neck.

Brachiocephalic: Flexes and turns the neck; extends the shoulder and front limbs.

Sternocephalicus: Flexes the head and neck.

Splenius: Extends the neck; supports/stabilizes the neck from above; bends the neck and head laterally.

Rhomboid: Lifts the shoulder up and forward; moves the scapula up, forward and back.

Trapezius cervicis: Lifts the shoulder; moves the scapula up and forward.

Rectus capitis muscle group: Flexes the poll; allows side movement of the head.

Multifidus cervicis: Flexes the neck and rotates the head; important spinal stabilizer.

Serratus ventralis cervicis: Extends and laterally flexes the neck; plays a major role in supporting the weight of the horse's trunk.

Omohyoid: Draws the chin to the chest.

Chest, Shoulder, and Forelimb

Unlike humans, horses do not have a collarbone, which means there are no bones or joints that attach the shoulder to the rib cage, only muscles. These muscles act as a "sling" and suspend the chest between the front legs. The muscles of the chest and shoulder are not only essential for stabilizing the front end, but have a direct influence on the swing of the front legs. The forelimb contains four joints: the shoulder, elbow, knee, and fetlock. Muscles end above the knee and the lower leg must rely on ligaments and tendons for stabilization. What follows are some of the most important muscles to keep in mind.

Superficial Muscles of the Shoulder

Trapezius thoracis: Moves shoulder up and back.

Deltoid: Flexes shoulder and moves the forelimb away from the midline (abduction).

Tricep: Flexes the shoulder joint; brings the front legs back; assists in elbow extension; stabilizes the front legs when at rest.

Deeper Muscles of the Shoulder

Infraspinatus: Extends and stabilizes the shoulder; abducts the shoulder.

Supraspinatus: Extends the shoulder.

Thoracic Sling

The *thoracic sling* is comprised of several muscles that work together to suspend the trunk between the scapula and front limbs. The front limbs are not attached to the skeleton by bone, but rather these muscles. The thoracic sling allows the chest to rise and lower between the shoulders like a spring and helps to rebalance the horse's weight from front to back. It is crucial for raising the sternum and withers in order to rock back on the hind end.

These muscles also allow for rotation of the trunk, which is essential for gait quality and balance. When the trunk is

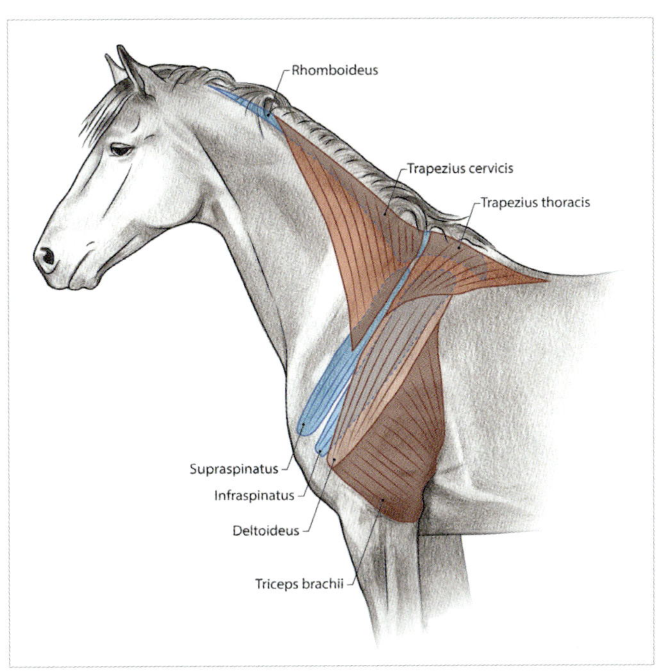

2.3 The shoulder muscles.

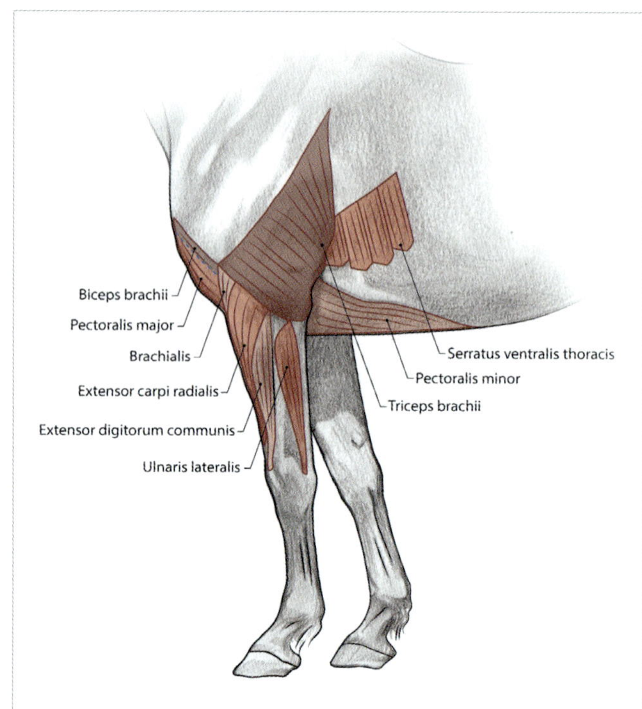

2.4 The chest and forelimbs.

stuck, the inside hip can't lower and move forward in a turn. Instead, the hind leg pushes out and the back muscles tighten.

The major muscles of the thoracic sling include the *serratus ventralis, pectorals,* and *subclavius* (fig. 2.4).

Serratus ventralis thoracis: Part of the *thoracic sling*, this is one of the largest muscles holding the chest between the limbs/attaching front limbs to trunk; draws scapula down and back helping to extend the limbs; helps create elasticity in the front end; lifts withers and raises rib cage.

Pectorals: Part of the thoracic sling, draws forelimbs forward, back, and toward the center (adduction).

Forelimb

Bicep: Extends the shoulder; flexes the elbow.

Tricep: Extends the elbow.

Brachialis: Flexes the elbow.

Extensor carpi radialis: Extends the knee joint; flexes the elbow.

Common digital extensor: Extends the knee and foot.

Ulnaris lateralis (Lateral Ulnar): Extends elbow; flexes knee.

Abdominals and Back

These muscles within the trunk make up the horse's core and are essential for supporting a rider (fig. 2.5).

Latissimus dorsi: This superficial muscle supports the back and allows lateral flexion of the spine; flexes the shoulder; retracts the front legs; works in opposition of the *brachiocephalicus.*

Longissimus dorsi: This deep muscle extends the back; supports lateral flexion; assists in exhalation.

Intercostals: Supports the ribs and assists in breathing.

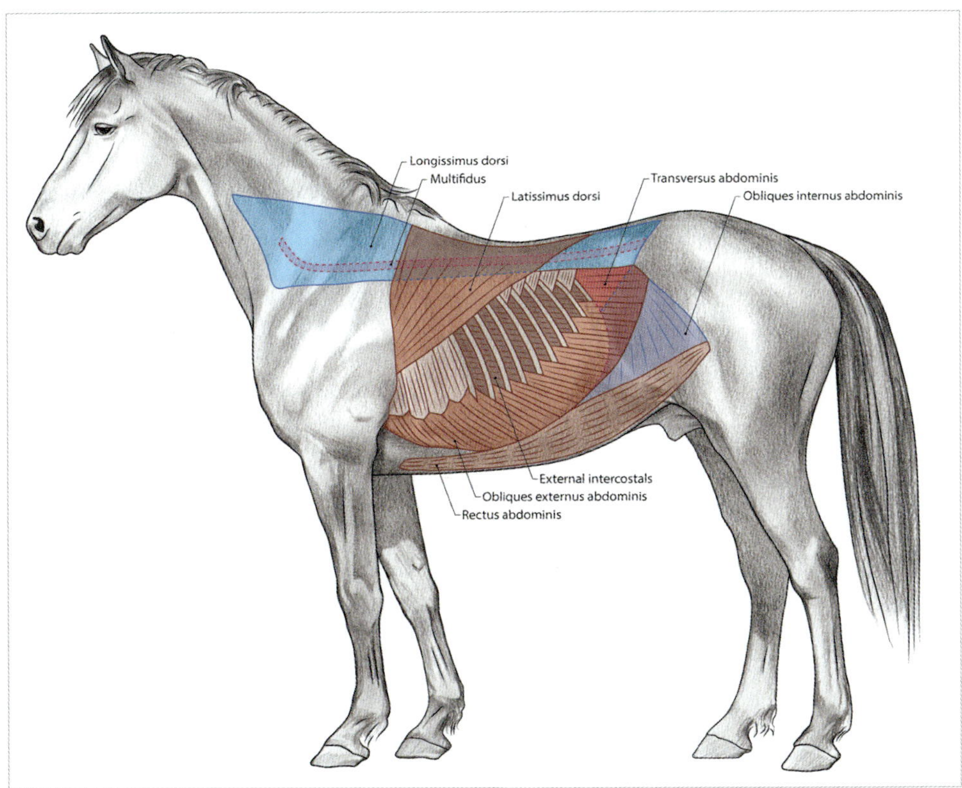

2.5 The abdominals and back, also known as the *core.*

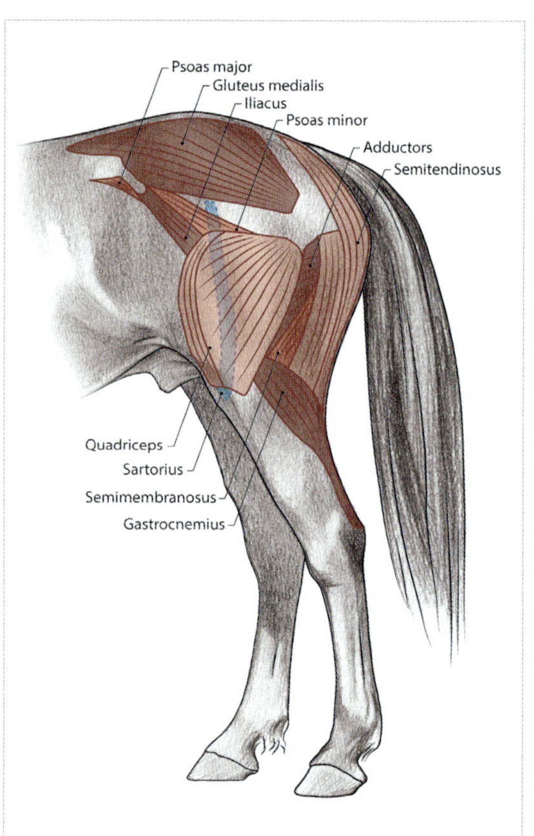

2.6 The muscles of the hindquarters.

***Obliques* (internal and external):** Essential for balance during forward motion; flexes the trunk laterally; draws the hind legs forward and under.

Rectus abdomius: Dorsiflexes and supports the back and organs.

Transverse abdominus: Deepest layer of abs, closest to the internal organs; essential for stabilization and breathing.

Multifidus: Stabilizes vertebrae and transfers power forward.

Hindquarters

The hindquarters are the motor for your horse (fig. 2.6 and see fig. 1.3, p. 17). Not only is it important to have powerful muscles in the hind end to drive forward locomotion, the muscles must be supple as well so that the horse can step up underneath himself to create true engagement.

Iliopsoas (psoas major and iliacus): Hip flexor; connects the trunk to the hindquarters enabling the legs to engage while stabilizing the spine and pelvis (aka posture); assists in hind leg protraction and outward rotation.

Psoas minor: Hip flexor.

Hamstring group: Hip extensors.
    Semimembranosus: Extends hip; adducts hock.
    Semitendinosus: Extends hip and hock;
    flexes stifle.
    Bicep femoris: Extends hind legs, hip, hock;
    flexes stifle.

Medial gluteal: Makes up a large portion of the top of the rump; point of origin is the *longissimus dorsi,* and they work together to lift the forehand; major hip extensor and abductor muscle.

Tensor fasciae latae: Flexes and abducts hip; extends stifle; originates from the hip bone and is responsible for a significant amount of fascia in the femur, which surrounds the stifle.

Sartorius: Flexes hip; moves the hind leg forward and inward (adduction); extends stifle.

Adductors: Adducts the limbs; retracts the limbs; moves the rump forward and sideways.

Quadriceps (Rectus femoris, vastus lateralis, vastus medialis, vastus intermedius): Flexes hip; extends stifle.

Gastrocnemius: Flexes stifle; extends hock.

Long digital extensor: Flexes hock; extends the hoof.

Lateral digital extensor: Extends the hoof.

Deep digital flexor tendon: Flexes the hoof.

Observation

Know Your Horse

Knowing your horse is the best thing you can do for preventive health therapy. You must get to know what is "normal" for your horse so that you'll be able to notice when things are off. It is also helpful to take note of your horse's current condition so you can track progress during training.

Observe Helpful Details

- Coat is shiny, not dull.

- Eyes are bright and attentive and horse alert.

- Nostrils are moist without discharge.

- No excessive heat or swelling in the limbs.

- Skin is easy to pull up and move back and forth, but also elastic and goes back to normal when released (sign of proper hydration).

- Good appetite.

- Sweating appropriately but not excessively. Sometimes a crooked horse will sweat only on one side or certain parts of the body that are overworked. Ideal sweat patterns should be around working muscles like the back, neck,

3.1 Your horse's topline is a good indicator of how well your training and nutrition program is working. This photo shows a "work in progress" as Mark was just coming back into work after EPM treatment when it was taken.

VITALS TO KNOW

- *Temperature* (normal is 99–101.5 Fahrenheit)
- *Pulse* (normal is 28–44 beats per minute, resting)
- *Weight*

Knowing your horse's normal pulse will help you create a program that is challenging in a safe and effective way. I use a heart-rate monitor to track my rides, making sure I haven't pushed my horse past his cardiovascular capabilities or stress threshold. Here you can see our jump session was well within the healthy limits of my horse's capabilities (fig. 3.2).

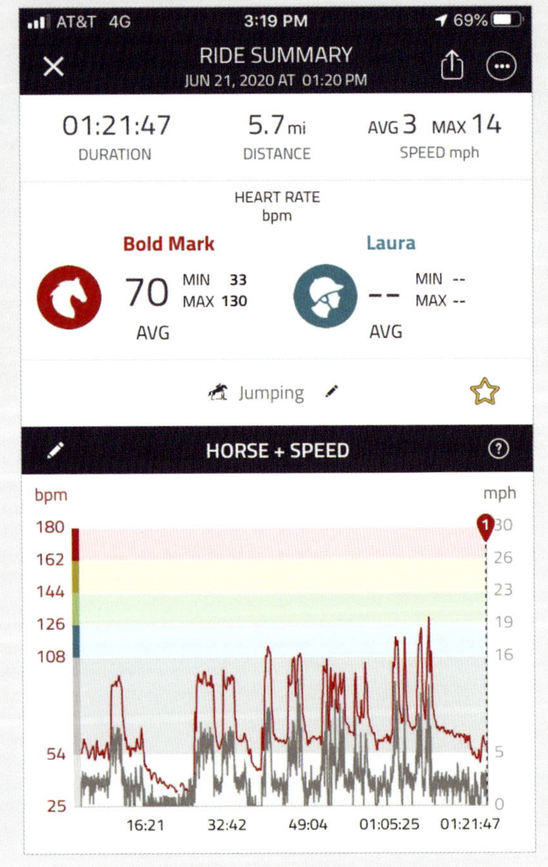

croup, and abs. The power muscles in the hind should work harder and sweat more, which typically means the flank and hip should be sweatier than the gaskin and stifle.

- Normal breathing should be around 12 to 18 breaths per minute. Under saddle, how long does it take the horse to blow through his nose? If your horse sighs when you let out the reins and stop work, this could be a sign of tension while moving.

- Body condition score:

  1 | Poor Extremely emaciated; shoulders, spinous processes, ribs and hips project prominently; no fatty tissue can be felt.

  2 | Very thin Emaciated; slight fat over spinous processes; ribs and hips are prominent; shoulders and withers are faintly discernable.

  3 | Thin Slight fat buildup on spinous processes but individual vertebrae cannot be seen; small amount of fat over ribs; hips appear round but easily discernable.

  4 | Moderately thin Faint outline of ribs; slight ridge along back; hip joints not discernable; shoulders, neck, and withers are not obviously thin.

5 | Moderate Back is flat; ribs can easily be felt but not seen; withers round over the spinous processes; shoulders and neck blend smoothly with the body.

6 | Moderately fleshy Fat over ribs feels spongy; fat deposits can be seen behind the shoulders and along the sides of the neck and withers; fat around tail head is soft.

7 | Fleshy Individual ribs can be felt but there is noticeable fat between them; fat along withers, behind shoulders and along neck; fat around tail head is soft.

8 | Fat Crease down back; difficult to feel ribs; fat around tail head is very soft; fat along withers, behind shoulders and along inner thighs; visible thickening of the neck.

9 | Extremely fat Obvious crease down back; patchy fat over ribs; bulging fat around tail head, along withers, behind shoulders and over neck; inner thighs are fat and possibly rubbing; flank filled with fat.

General Guidelines for Conformation

You already have your horse, so don't dwell on conformation faults. What you should note during observation is a baseline "normal" to create training goals from and reference later to assess changes (figs. 3.3 and 3.4).

Front View

- Eyes and nostrils are horizontal; is the head crooked from tension somewhere?

- Muscles of neck (*brachiocephalicus*), shoulder (*triceps*), chest (*pectorals*), lower arm (*extensors and flexors*) are even.

- Forelegs are holding equal weight and are lined up properly with the shoulders. If the horse stands slightly too wide or narrow this could mean muscular tension in the neck and/or shoulders that can be addressed through work.

3.3 Here you can see my horse Mark's left shoulder is lower and thicker, and his neck is a little tighter on the left side (partly because he is not standing square and is distracted, but also due to tightness). We can use this knowledge to stretch the lateral neck muscles on the left and begin encouraging more strengthening on the right. The pectorals and legs are moderately balanced.

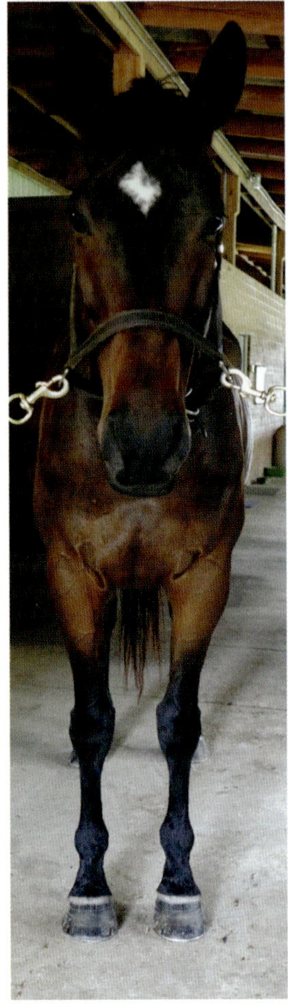

3.4 It's important to look closely at your horse from top to bottom. Here you can see Mark is alert and his ears are forward and attentive. His face is balanced but his stance is slightly narrow, which could mean tight adductor muscles. He is standing equally in both front feet.

Side View

- Equal weight distributed between the front and hind legs and between the topline and underside/flexor chain.

- Angle between head and neck is roughly 90 degrees and the head is relaxed.

- Neck musculature should be even with no dip in the front of the shoulder blade (space between nuchal ligament and cervical spine is filled in).

- Forelegs are perpendicular to the ground. Can you draw a plumb line from the middle of the shoulder blade, through the elbow, to the middle of the knee and down to the backside of the heel bulb?

- Abdominals are naturally taut and not hanging or tense.

- Hind legs are perpendicular. Can you draw a plumb line from the seat bone to the rear edge of the hock and fetlock?

Issues to Note from the Side

- Front legs too far forward can mean pain in a lower limb or tension in the shoulder.

- Front legs too far behind can mean tension in the cervical spine.

- Hind legs too far under the body can mean tightness in the lumbar area or back pain.

- Hind legs too far back can mean issues with lifting the back due to pain or tension.

3.5 Here you can see Mark's side view before beginning a new training program. His abdominals are tight, his coat is healthy, and his head is relaxed. He could use some more even muscling in the neck and a stronger back and hind end, which will bring his legs under him a little more. Again, look more for balance and musculature than for overall conformation faults.

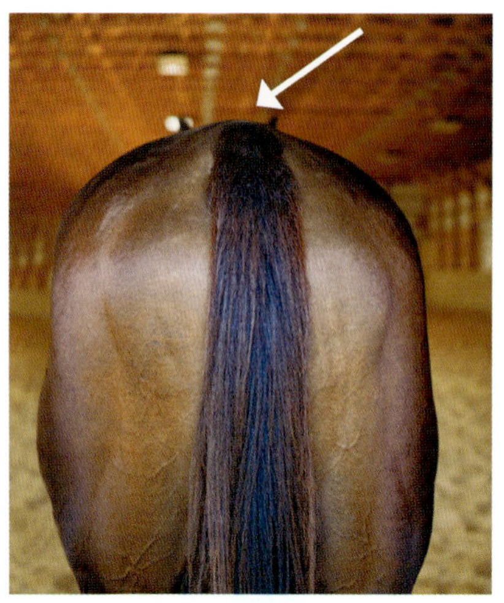

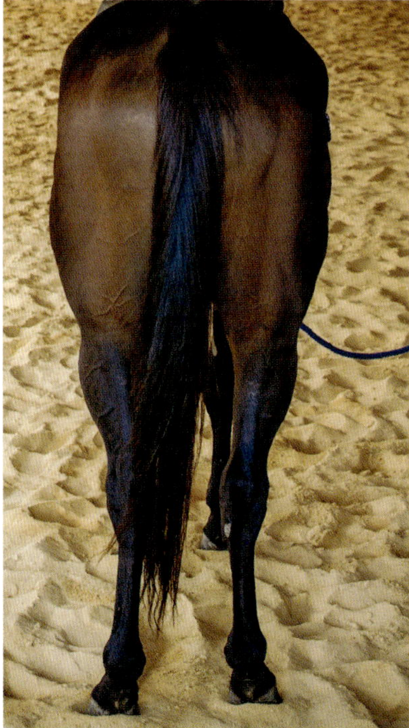

Hind View

One of the most common issues with horses is subluxation, or "hunter's bump." When the sacroiliac joint has lost its normal position, you may see what looks like an "A" shape or a point at the center of the hind end (fig. 3.6). A strong and healthy horse butt should look more like a heart shape with two strong gluteals rounding on either side of the spine (fig. 3.7). Other important observations from behind:

- Even muscling on both sides.

- Muscles around the stifle should be widest part of the horse. If not, they may need some extra strengthening work.

- Base of support:
  - Narrow-based horses need more strengthening in the legs due to additional stress on the bones and joints. There is also increased potential for interference—make sure to use boots when training. Consider that your horse may be standing narrow due to tight adductor muscles or because of pelvis or hip pain.

  - Bow-legged horses sometimes have trouble accessing their hindquarters power and struggle to push from behind properly. They need more time working the hind-end muscles.

- Wide-based horses tend to overload the joints of the lower leg, particularly on the inside. Consider that your horse may be standing wide due to a tight croup or hamstring muscles.

Bird's Eye View

This is the best way to check for muscle balance in the shoulders and hips and along the spine. Stand on a mounting block to get a good view of your horse's back (fig. 3.8).

In Movement

- Head is relaxed, slightly low and swings back and forth.
  - If the head is too low, your horse may have issues bearing weight on the hind.
  - An unstable head and neck position can reveal unstable weight placement through the legs.
- Shoulder blades glide up and down, moving evenly.
- Both front legs reach the same height; both hind legs reach the same height.
- Trunk swings to the sides evenly.
- Hind legs follow the front legs in single lines.
- Even weight distribution side-to-side.

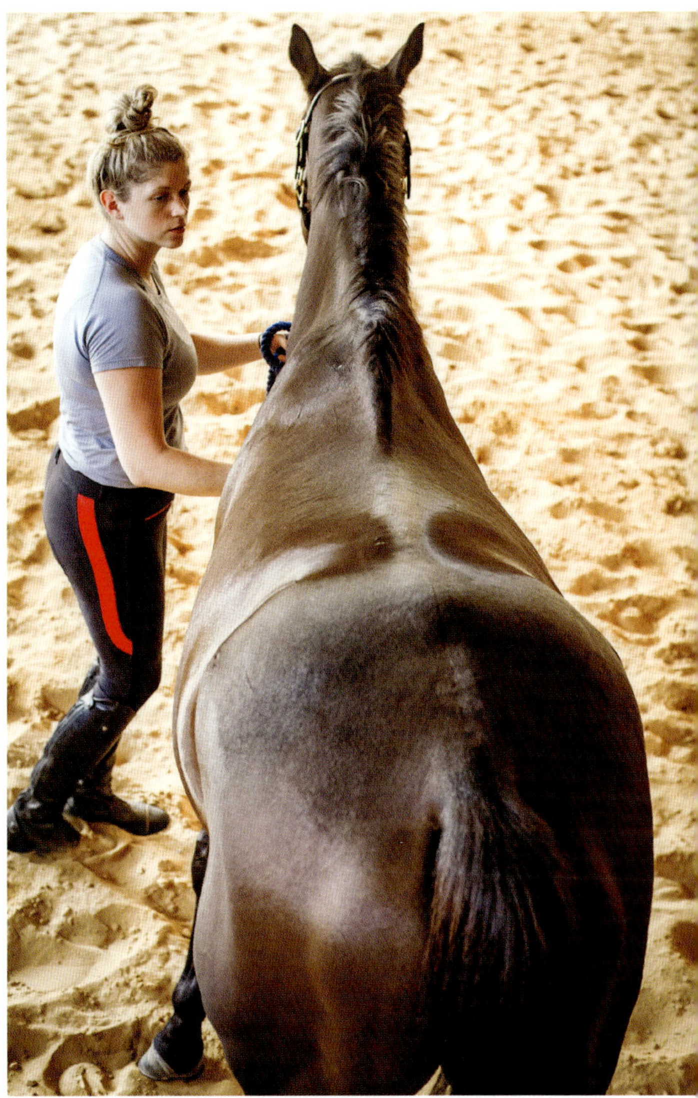

3.8 Notice Mark's left shoulder blade is higher and wider, and the right gluteal is weaker. This means the front left leg is bearing more weight and there could be tension in the cervical vertebrae or the first thoracic vertebra.

- Front legs should reach out and forward during movement then stabilize during the weight bearing phase. If your horse is too heavy on the forehand, the legs may bear weight even when extending fully forward or when reaching back.

- As your horse's weight shifts back, the joints should flex and bend.

- The hind legs should be straight down from a neutral pelvis. When moving, the pelvis should rotate up at the front and down at the back to allow the hind legs to reach forward and under.

- The back should be supple and go through a full range of motion, lifting back to front and bottom to top. It must also lift the front end to allow mobility in the front legs.

- Horse should not appear more developed in the front muscles than in the rear.

Know Your Saddle Fit

Saddle fit is something many riders struggle with and can often be a source of back pain if overlooked or incorrect. Your saddle should be checked twice a year by a professional, but more often when the horse is changing due to a strength and conditioning program.

When was the last time you had your saddle's flocking checked or ran your hands along the panels on the underside of your saddle? Use this check-list as a guide to see if it's time to make a change with your saddle fit (figs. 3.10 A & B).

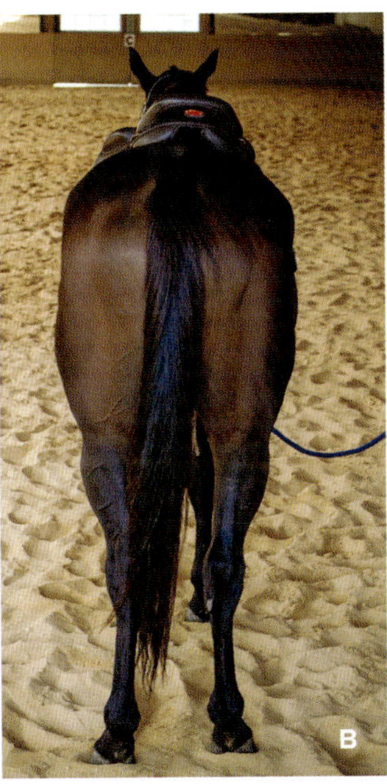

3.10 A & B After trying numerous saddles, a wool-flocked adjustable tree Hastilow Concept fit Mark best. This is great for a horse undergoing big muscular changes because you can adjust both the flocking and the width of the tree. The saddle fit is balanced using a shimmable half pad with pads in the front left and back right panels to help level the saddle while working toward better symmetry (A). Without a half pad, Mark's saddle has slightly rotated and dropped on the right (B). If a rider were to sit in this saddle, she automatically would be tipped right, placing more weight on that side of the body and throwing off the horse's balance.

- Place the saddle on your horse's back without a pad, and run your hand along the panel underneath the side flap, where it meets the horse's back. The entire length of the panel should lie evenly against your horse's back and feel smooth without noticeable softness in the middle. Check both sides.

- Gullet (space between panels) should be at least two-to-three-fingers wide to allow room for the spine. Your saddle should not be sitting on the horse's spine.

- Panels must lie evenly on the horse's back from behind, and the back of the saddle shouldn't lift when pressure is placed on the pommel or when the girth is tightened.

- You should be able to fit three fingers between the withers and the pommel.

- The middle of the saddle should be the deepest point.

- Saddle should lie behind the shoulder blade so it doesn't impede shoulder mobility.

- Saddle should not sit farther back than the end of the thoracic vertebrae.

- A half pad can be useful; however, everything placed between a saddle and the horse's back will make the saddle more narrow and create potential for compression. As explained by a saddle fitter, this can be likened to wearing a sock with a high heel.

- Make sure the girth is long enough so the elbow doesn't bump the buckle.

Know Yourself

Wearing a shirt with stripes makes observing your posture easier, but it's not necessary. Check and pad the saddle as necessary for it to sit evenly on your horse (see p. 45). Have someone take a picture of you from behind when your horse is standing squarely on level ground.

The photo will show you if you're sitting crookedly in the saddle, which forces the horse to compensate for your own imbalances. When you sit asymmetrically, the horse's muscles on the opposite side of the weight tend to tense up in order to balance out the heavier side (fig. 3.11).

It is also a good idea to have someone video tape you riding on a circle in both directions, doing both upward and downward transitions. This will give you an idea of how evenly and balanced you are sitting in the saddle. We cannot ask our horse to be perfectly balanced if we do not also work on ourselves. Can you stand in the stirrups with your arms out to a "T" for an entire circle around the arena? If not, spend some time working without stirrups, in two-point, and on the ground doing core and balance exercises.

Know What Your Horse is Eating

Asking your vet for comprehensive bloodwork, including a complete blood count and chemistry analysis, is an excellent idea at the beginning of a new training program. This ensures your horse is getting adequate fuel for both building muscle and maintaining overall health. Just as most people get a physical and a full blood workup every year, or at least are supposed to, these tests are an important tool to keep an eye on your horse's wellness and make sure he is not missing any key nutrients.

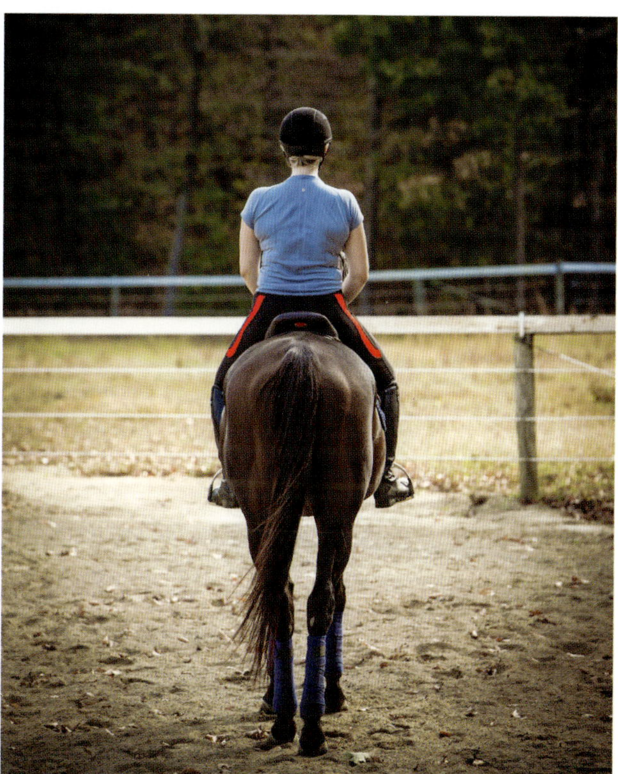

3.11 Mark is not standing squarely so this is not a perfect representation of checking rider balance; however, you can see the right side of my body is slightly shorter that the left. I need to drop my left shoulder and place a little more weight into my right hip to create more evenness in my body.

A general rule to follow is that a horse should get roughly 2.5 to 3 percent of his body weight in food per day with as much being forage as possible—roughly 80 percent hay, 20 percent grain. In an ideal situation, your horse should have access to forage 24/7, and each grain-based meal should weigh between 2 to 4 pounds (including alfalfa cubes, beet pulp, and other supplements). Keep in mind that as work increases, more fuel will be burned: a working horse typically needs more calories than a horse at rest. If your horse gains weight however, this can increase pressure on the joints and create heat in the body leading to fatigue.

Adequate, high-quality protein intake is important for muscle growth and repair. Protein is made of amino acids, and lysine, methionine, and threonine are the most important amino acids to consider when working to fill out your horse's topline and overall musculature. Horses only need about 1.4 to 2.15 pounds of protein a day, most of which is amply provided by good forage (grass and hay) and a small amount of grain; however, some people have found that

BLOODWORK EXAMPLE

Here is an example of some of the bloodwork done for Mark before starting a new training program. This blood was pulled while Mark was on 10,000IUs of vitamin E, selenium, Purina Outlast, SmartImmune, and probiotics. You can easily see that the test results all came back within "normal" range. All you have to do is Google the test name—or ask your vet—to see which nutrients you may need to keep an eye on. For example, "GLU" stands for glucose, or blood sugar, and it's in the lower part of normal range, so I will remember to keep an eye on it. In the meantime, after talking to an equine nutritionist, I added hemp, flax, colostrum, salt, and a joint supplement to my horse's diet.

Test	Results	Reference Interval
VetTest		
GLU	69 mg/dL	64 - 150
CREA	1.3 mg/dL	0.8 - 2.2
BUN	14 mg/dL	10 - 25
CA	11.5 mg/dL	10.4 - 12.9
TP	6.4 g/dL	5.6 - 7.9
ALB	2.8 g/dL	1.9 - 3.2
GLOB	3.6 g/dL	2.4 - 4.7
AST	343 U/L	100 - 600
ALKP	203 U/L	10 - 326
GGT	37 U/L	0 - 87
TBIL	0.7 mg/dL	0.0 - 3.5
CK	192 U/L	10 - 350
LDH	642 U/L	250 - 2070

LOW   NORMAL   HIGH

an amino acid supplement can help build topline muscles even when their horse is out of work.

Omega-3 fatty acids and natural vitamin E are also important additions to a working horse's diet for their anti-inflammatory benefits. These nutrients help repair muscle damage and alleviate fatigue. Consider adding supplements such as ¼ cup of hemp, flax, or chia seeds to your horse's feed as a way to increase protein and omegas.

Water and proper hydration is crucial for all horses. Blood is made predominantly of water, and therefore, water is needed to transport nutrients to cells, regulate body temperature, and help lubricate the joints. It's also necessary for removing waste from the body. Horses need between 5 to 15 gallons of water a day. Make sure your horse has access to fresh water at all times, and consider adding electrolytes—a salt block is good, but a few tablespoons of free salt in the feed, especially in the summer, can help with hydration. Test your horse's hydration by pinching some skin on his neck and then releasing it. The skin should go back to normal within two seconds if the horse is properly hydrated.

It's also very important to make sure your horse doesn't get an excessive amount of sugary treats, especially when doing incentive stretches daily. Cooling treats such as mint, broccoli, and celery can be good substitutions for molasses-based treats. There are also probiotic treats available, as well as omega treats.

Know When to Get Started

Now that you know more about your horse and yourself, you're ready to start working safely and effectively. Use this book as a guide and feel free to tailor exercises as you and your horse need.

The photos in the exercises to follow are not perfect. They are a representation of a young ex-racehorse recovering from EPM, working toward a stronger and more balanced body after months of muscle atrophy and nerve damage. Please keep in mind that these exercises are a work in progress for us, and hopefully for you and your horse, as well. Pilates is a journey for all of us.

Exercises

The following exercises are presented in a training manual format to give you an idea of not only what each exercise is, but how to do it and why. Pilates professionals are taught to not only memorize exercises and choreography, but to know the practical applications and benefit, or "why," behind each movement. When you know the purpose, remembering how to do the exercise becomes much easier. As always, introduce new exercises to your horse slowly and in a safe and calm environment.

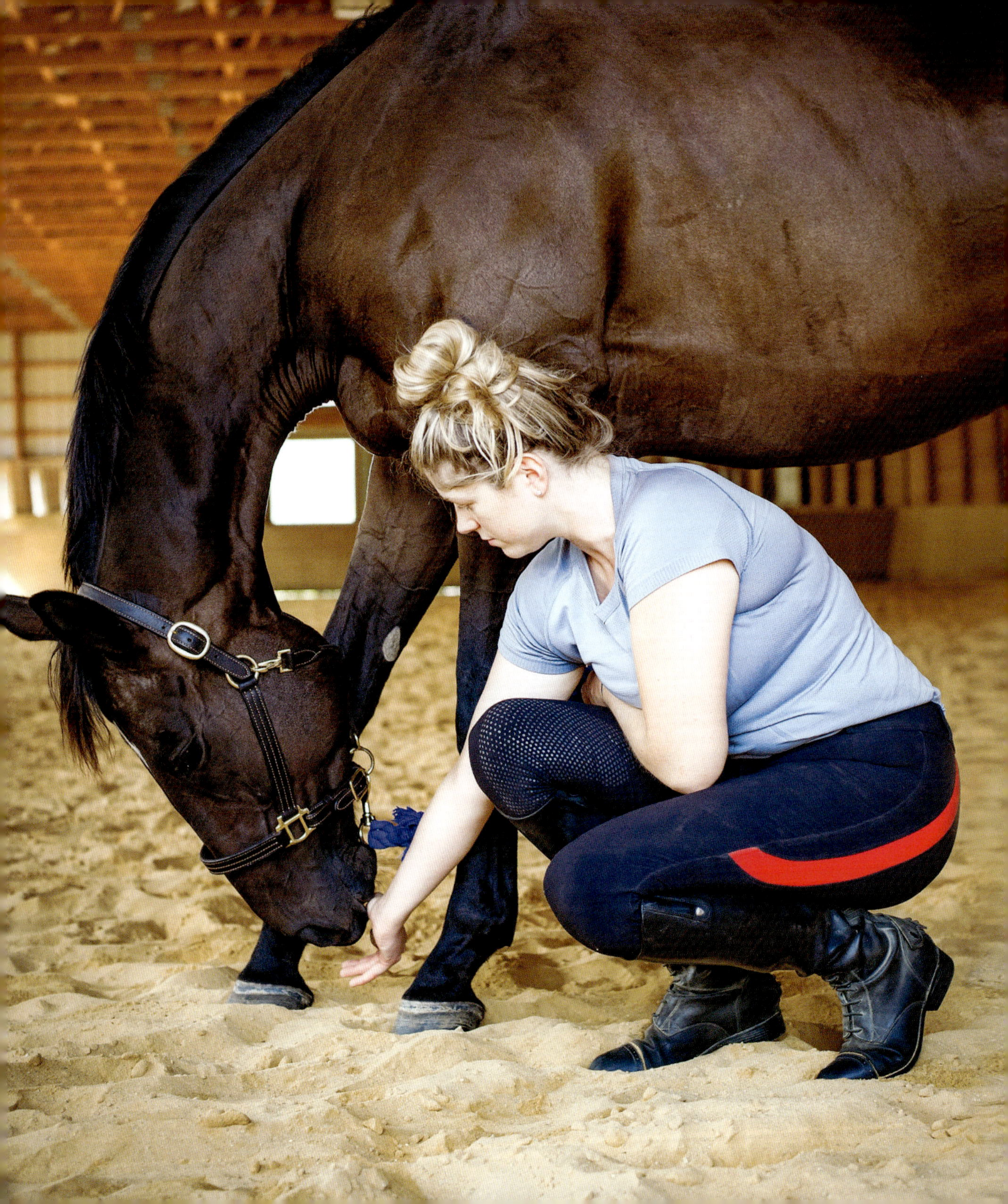

chapter 4

Stretching

Human athletes know that stretching is an invaluable part of any training program to keep muscles elastic, and a tight muscle is more prone to injury. Stretching helps to improve circulation, range of motion, and overall health of your horse's muscles, while also decreasing muscle soreness and fatigue. As an added benefit, spending a few minutes stretching your horse can help create a stronger bond.

WHAT

The three main stretches covered in this book—*incentive stretches, supported static hold stretches,* and *dynamic mobilization stretches*—are all techniques that pull your horse's various limbs and muscles into a lengthened state to help increase mobility and flexibility, and release tension. When strengthening muscles, it's important to also lengthen them to maintain suppleness.

Incentive stretches (p. 55) require the use of a treat or "incentive" to get your horse to stretch into a lengthened state on his own.

Supported static hold stretches (p. 66) require a handler to support the weight of the horse's limb as it is pulled into a stretch.

Dynamic mobilization stretches (p. 77) increase range of motion through supported movements of the horse's body.

4.1 Incentive stretches, one of the three types of stretches described in the following pages, use treats or "incentives" to allow the horse to stretch himself. By elongating the neck, the back will also stretch and the core will engage to stabilize, making this a full-body exercise.

STRETCH INTENSITY

The intensity of a stretch is considered the amount of force used to elongate the muscle, and less intensity is needed than you might think. Using too much force may strain or otherwise injure healthy tissue; keeping the intensity of these stretches to a light pull will be most beneficial for your horse.

WHY

- Increases range of motion, suppleness, and stride length.

- Reduces muscle soreness.

- Helps prevent muscle and joint strain.

- Eases tension in both the body and mind.

- Increases body awareness and proprioception.

- Engages stabilizers, increasing balance.

- Increases circulation.

WHEN

- The benefit of stretching before work is that the horse will be more loose and supple for the riding session to come, but the muscles will be cold and mobility won't be as accessible within the stretches. There is also a greater chance of strain when stretching before warming up. It is best to complete a stretching routine *after* work, as part of your horse's cool-down.

- Ideally, stretches should be performed three to four times a week to prevent tightness.

- Hold each stretch for 10–20 seconds, especially when introducing a new technique, and work up to 45 seconds. Repeat 3–4 times on each side.

Common Issues and Precautions

- As with a human, too much mobility (hypermobility) can cause issues. If your horse can easily move into a full range of motion, strengthening the surrounding muscles of that joint should be prioritized over stretching.

Incentive Stretches

WHAT

Also known as "carrot stretches," incentive stretches use treats or a clicker to ask your horse to stretch himself through flexion (rounding), lateral bending (side to side), and even extension (hollowing or reaching).

WHY

- Stretches the neck and back, increasing range of motion and suppleness.

- Improves strength and stability—especially in the core and topline.

- Reduces risk of injury.

- Increases bond between rider and horse.

TOOLS

- Treats. I don't recommend using big carrots because horses can grab and hold them, engaging the jaw and neck muscles, which creates tension instead of release. A treat that your horse is overly fond of will make it harder to maintain his attention and more likely that he will lunge with his teeth. Find a food low in artificial sugar such as apple slices, celery, or smaller chunks of carrot to use. Low sugar Omega Nibblers® are also a great option.

- Gloves.

- Clicker if your horse becomes nippy.

WHEN

Stretches may be done every day, ideally after work when your horse's muscles are warm.

tips for Incentive Stretches

- ➤ Stand close to the horse and out of kicking range.

- ➤ Do not try stretches in an enclosed space like a wash stall; make sure there is room to step away if your horse loses balance.

- ➤ Don't use the cross-ties when asking your horse to stretch. Ask a friend to hold the horse, perform the stretches in a big stall, or ground tie.

- ➤ If your horse tries to step back to follow the treat instead of stretching, ask for the stretch in front of a wall or have a friend place her hand on the horse's hind end to discourage backward movement. Be patient and let your horse figure out what you're asking.

- ➤ Don't force these stretches. Allow the horse to be in control and do not pull him into position or hold his head down. Your horse is most likely already working hard to get the treat and needs time and repetition in order to go deeper in this position.

- ➤ Try different treats to see what works best. If you pick something your horse loves, like a Stud Muffin, he may lunge for the treat or become nippy.

- ➤ If your horse becomes nippy, especially when not asking for the stretch, spend some time training him to respond to a clicker.

Chin to Chest

WHAT

Ask your horse to bring his nose toward the center of his chest using a treat, creating flexion and stretch in the upper neck muscles.

WHY

- Increases mobility in the upper and middle neck muscles including the *trapezius cervicis*, *cervical rhomboids*, and *splenius* muscles.

HOW

1 Stand beside your horse, facing forward.

2 Offer a treat near the horse's nose to get his attention.

3 Slowly move your hand back toward the center of the horse's chest, covering the treat so he cannot grab it.

4 Make sure the horse's neck is straight and his nose is pointing down.

5 When using a clicker, activate it right at the center of your horse's chest.

6 Hold the stretch for 5 seconds to start, working up to 10–20 seconds over the course of several weeks.

7 Repeat 2–4 times, changing sides each time so your horse's head doesn't begin to tilt to one side in anticipation (figs. 4.2 A & B).

WHEN

Every day, after your horse is warmed up. Hold for 10–20 seconds and repeat 2–4 times.

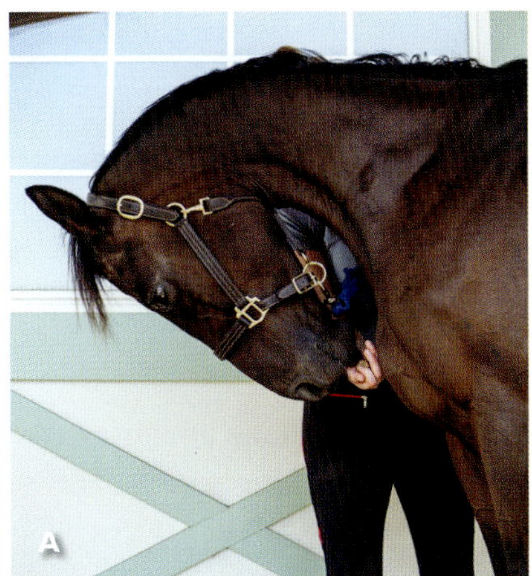

4.2 A & B Mark is stretching his upper neck muscles (A). Even though he is stretching straight down, I make sure to repeat the stretch standing on both sides to discourage any tilt of the head or neck. Notice I have my fingers closed around a treat so Mark stays interested and cannot grab the treat with his teeth (B). I trust that I can move quickly if Mark tries to bite the treat out of my hand, but this is not advised if your horse tends to lunge for treats.

Common Issues and Precautions

- When you hold the treat too high, the neck and jaw will tense, and the horse will not get the full benefit of the stretch. Holding the incentive at the middle of the chest elongates the muscles down the neck and through the back instead of just the poll.

- Refer to pages 54 and 55 for more tips on this and other *incentive stretches*. Never hold your horse's head down or force him into a greater range of motion than he offers.

WHAT

Ask your horse to bring his nose down toward his knees and eventually between them using a treat, flexing and stretching the neck and back.

WHY

- Increases mobility and encourages deep flexion of the middle and lower neck muscles including the *rectus capitus lateralis, multifidus cervicis,* and *serratus ventralis cervicis.*

- Stretches the topline, loosening the *rhomboids* and *trapezius* muscles that wrap around the spinous processes at the withers.

- Strengthens flexion at the poll.

HOW

1 Stand to the side of your horse, facing forward.

2 Offer a treat near the horse's nose to get his attention.

3 Slowly move your hand back toward the knees. If your horse is already flexible in this area, you can reach your hand behind your horse's elbow and forward toward his nose, slowly pulling the treat back to the knees and then farther, between the knees and toward the belly.

4 Make sure your horse's neck is straight, the nose is pointing down, and he is standing squarely with the front legs.

5 When using a clicker, activate it right between the horse's knees.

6 Hold for 5 seconds to start, working up to 10–20 seconds over the course of several weeks.

7 Repeat 2–4 times, changing sides each time so your horse doesn't begin to tilt to one side in anticipation (fig. 4.3).

Every day, after your horse is warmed up. Hold for 10–20 seconds and repeat 2–4 times.

Common Issues and Precautions

- It's okay for your horse's knees to bend, but this can be a compensation that takes away from the stretch. Start by asking for less of a stretch and work into a deeper flexion slowly.

- Refer to pages 54 and 55 for more tips and precautions.

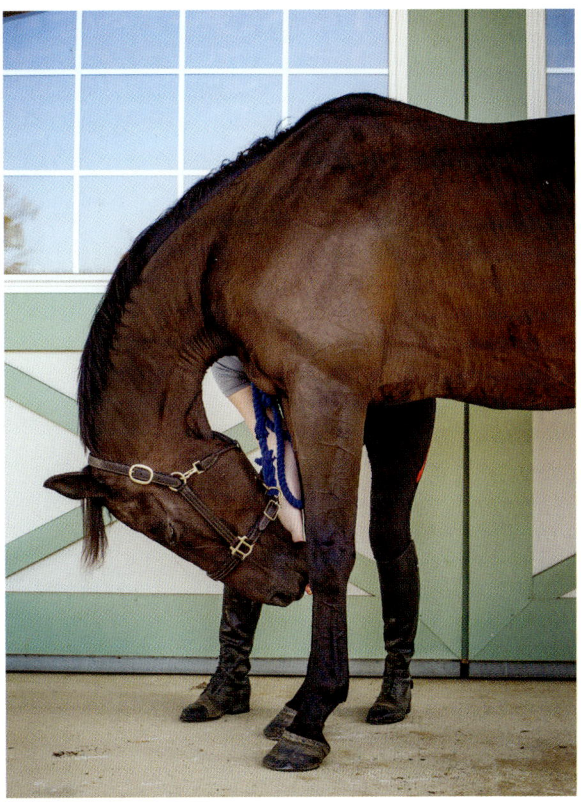

4.3 This stretch elongates the mid and lower neck muscles as well as the entire topline of the body. Notice Mark's knees are straight, he is standing squarely, and he is reaching straight down.

Nose to Toes

WHAT

Ask your horse to bring his nose down toward his front feet using a treat, flexing and stretching the neck and back.

WHY

- Increases mobility and encourages deep flexion of the *rhomboid* muscle as well as the lower neck muscles including the *brachiocephalicus, sternocephalicus* and the *omohyoid* muscle.

- Stretches the back, especially through the thoracic region.

- Activates stabilizers in both the front and hind end and engages the *abdominals*.

HOW

1 Stand to the side of your horse, facing forward.

2 Offer a treat right in front of your horse's nose to get his attention.

3 Slowly move your hand back toward the body and down toward the ground. If the horse is already flexible in this area, you can reach your hand behind the elbow and forward toward the nose, slowly pulling the treat down to the feet and then back between them.

4 Make sure your horse's neck is straight, the nose is pointing down, and he is standing squarely with the front legs.

5 When using a clicker, activate it directly between the front feet.

6 Hold for 5 seconds to start, working up to 10–20 seconds over the course of several weeks.

7 Repeat 2–4 times, changing sides each time to give the muscles time to recover (fig. 4.4).

WHEN

Every day, after your horse is warmed up. Hold for 10–20 seconds and repeat 2–4 times.

Common Issues and Precautions

- Don't allow your horse to flex too much at the poll. Ask the horse to reach out and then down.

- It's okay for your horse's knees to bend but this can be a compensation that takes away from the stretch. Start by asking for less of a stretch and work into a deeper flexion slowly.

- Refer to pages 54 and 55 for more tips and precautions.

Nose to Girth

WHAT

Ask your horse to laterally bend and stretch as he reaches for a treat at his side.

WHY

- Encourages lateral bend and stretches the muscles on the side of the neck and back including the *splenius, multifidus cervicis, serratus ventralis, trapezius, serratus thoracis, latissiumus dorsi, longissimus dorsi, scalene muscles, intercostals* and *obliques.*

- Strengthens the *pectoral stabilizer muscles* and *obliques.*

HOW

1 Stand next to your horse's shoulder, facing away from him.

2 Offer a treat with your outside hand near the horse's nose to get his attention.

3 Slowly move your hand around your body and toward the horse's hip, asking for a stretch.

4.5 A & B In A, I am supporting Mark's neck as he stretches around me. This is the most gentle form of the stretch. You can also accomplish this stretch standing slightly farther away from your horse, as I am in B. This encourages the inside scapula to draw backward and the *obliques* to engage, but increases the risk for compression if you ask for too deep of a stretch.

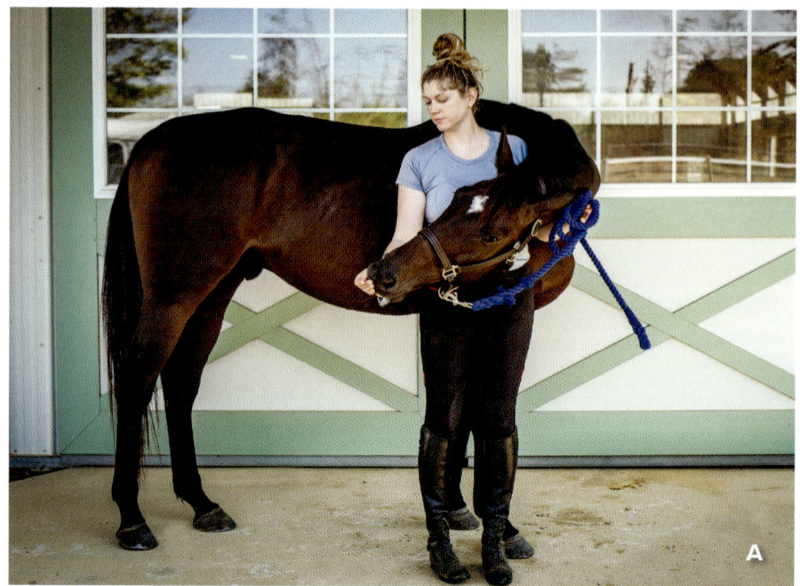

4 Support the outside of the neck lightly with your inside hand and maintain a consistent neck height no higher than the hip.

5 When using a clicker, activate it at the back half of your horse's trunk,
   halfway down the side.

6 Make sure your horse is not tilting his head and is standing square if
   possible.

7 Hold for 5 seconds to start, working up to 10–20 seconds over the
   course of several weeks.

8 Repeat 3–4 times, changing sides each time to give the muscles time to
   recover (figs. 4.5 A & B).

WHEN

Every day, after your horse is warmed up. Hold for 10–20 seconds and repeat
2–4 times.

Common Issues and Precautions

- If you think your horse may potentially lose his balance or bite
  you, stand a few feet away from the shoulder and ask the horse
  to stretch directly back. Avoid too tight of a bend as this can
  cause lower cervical spine compression.

- Keep in mind that horses can and will use their teeth to scratch
  their hind end naturally, especially during fly season. By standing
  next to the trunk and asking the horse to stretch his neck around
  you, you can encourage the horse to shift his shoulder out,
  engage the *core*, and hold a deep lateral bend of the opposite side
  of the body.

- Refer to pages 54 and 55 for more tips and precautions.

WHAT

Ask your horse to laterally bend and flex down as he reaches for a treat outside of each front foot.

WHY

- Encourages lateral bend and stretches the lateral (side) muscles of the neck and thoracolumbar spine including the *scalenus, multifidus cervicis, braciocephalicus, rectus capitis dorsalis, lateralis* and *serratus muscles.*

- Activates the *abdominals* and *pelvic stabilizers.*

HOW

1 Stand to the side of your horse, facing forward.

2 Offer a treat right in front of your horse's nose to get his attention.

3 Slowly move your hand back toward the shoulder and down toward the outside of the hoof closest to you.

4 The nose should face down and not sideways toward the treat, but do not force straightness with your hands.

5 Hold for 5 seconds to start, working up to 10–20 seconds over the course of several weeks.

6 Repeat 2–4 times, changing sides each time to give the muscles time to recover (figs. 4.6 A & B).

WHEN

Every day, after your horse is warmed up. Hold for 10–20 seconds and repeat 2–4 times.

Common Issues and Precautions

- Ask your horse to stretch laterally before moving downward to encourage bend in the neck and not the knees.

- Refer to pages 54 and 55 for more tips and precautions.

4.6 A & B In this stretch, I am asking for just a slight lateral bend (A). Mark has a tendency to lose his balance in this stretch and buckle his knees so I ask for a smaller range of motion and stay prepared to move quickly if necessary. In the other direction, you can see Mark shift his weight back slightly, engaging his core (B). I would prefer his left hind leg to be down and not rested; however, he is still getting a stretch through the right side of the body.

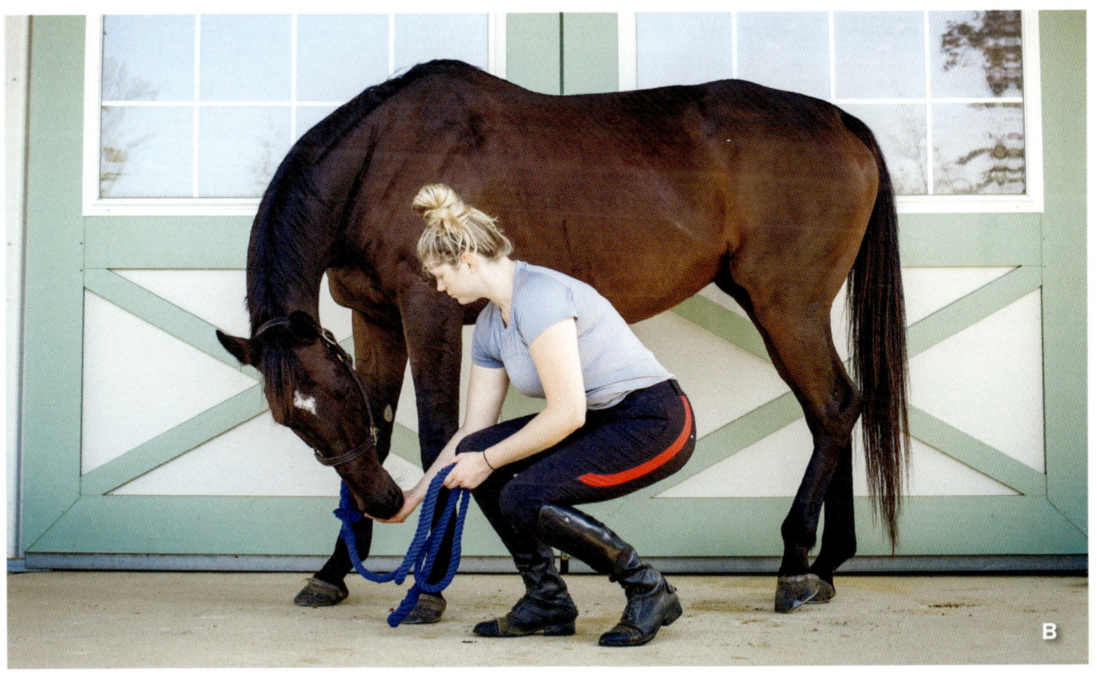

Supported Static Hold Stretches

WHAT

In these stretches, you assist your horse by holding his limbs or body in a gentle, supported, elongated position, allowing the muscles to relax and lengthen. A *static hold stretch* is one where a single position is held for a period of time, usually around 30-45 seconds.

WHY

- Increases length of muscles, promoting greater range of motion and ease of movement.

- Loosens and supples the body.

- Increases balance.

TOOLS

- Having an assistant can be helpful.

WHEN

These stretches can be done every day after muscles are warm and relaxed.

Tail Pull Back

WHAT

By gently pulling backward on your horse's tail, you can put his spine in traction, allowing for spinal decompression and pressure relief. The horse may also shift his weight forward against the pressure, elongating the spine, and engaging the *abdominals*.

WHY

- This isometric contraction stretches the stabilizing muscles along the spine, freeing the back and relieving tension in the topline muscles including the *longissimus dorsi* and *latissimus dorsi* as well as the *gluteals* and *trapezius thoracis*.

- Engages the *abdominals* if the horse shifts his balance away from your pressure.

HOW

1 Stand behind your horse and gently lift the dock of his tail until it's lined up with the spine or just below it.

2 Hold the tail steady until your horse releases tension/clamping feeling.

3 Slide your hands down the tail and take a few steps back.

4 Slowly pull the tail directly backward. Your horse may shift forward against you, which will increase the stretch and engage his stabilizer muscles.

tips **for Tail Pull Back**

➤ If your horse is prone to kicking, skip this exercise or make sure to stand sufficiently far back.

➤ The goal is for your horse to shift his weight forward and activate the lower line of the body while releasing his topline. However, it is still beneficial as a stretch if your horse does not shift his weight.

➤ Step one foot back so you can brace your body for any movement that might occur without falling over.

4.7 A It's important to lift the dock of the tail slowly and wait for the horse to unclamp or release tension before pulling back.

5 Hold for 10–20 seconds to start, working up to a minute if your horse allows, over time (figs. 4.7 A & B).

WHEN

Every day, before or after work. Hold for 10 seconds to a minute.

Common Issues and Precautions

- If your horse refuses to unclamp his tail, try placing three fingers where the dock meets the body and press down gently. If that doesn't work, raise the tail only halfway and spend time gently massaging the dock with the pads of your fingers and/or moving the dock slowly in small circles to release tension.

- If you cannot get your horse to release his tail, move on to **Lacrosse Ball Release** (p. 172), and if the tail is still tense afterward, this may be an indication that a chiropractor or veterinarian should look at your horse.

WHAT

In this supported stretch, you will hold your horse's hind leg while stretching it back away from the body. This is considered a *retraction* stretch, meaning the limb is being pulled backward from the center of the body.

WHY

- Stretches the muscles of the hind end and back including the *gluteal* muscles, *bicep femoris, rectus femoris, tensor fascia latae, semimembranosus, semitendinosus, long digital extensor, lateral digital extensor, quadriceps* and *obliques.*

- Reduces muscle stiffness in the pelvis and increases range of motion in the hind legs, which can increase stride length.

HOW TO

1 Stand beside your horse, facing back, and pick up a back foot as if picking the hoof.

2 Support the fetlock as you slowly walk back in a straight line, stretching—or *retracting*—the leg away from the body.

3 Move slowly, continuing to support and stretch the leg back until you feel a slight tension against the stretch. Pause and allow the muscles to release.

4 Hold for 15–30 seconds before walking forward to release the stretch. Gently place the leg down.

5 You can rest the horse's leg on your inside knee, but always be prepared for him to pull away suddenly.

6 Repeat for the same amount of time on each side (figs. 4.8 A & B).

tips **for Hind Leg Reach Back**

➤ This stretch is best with warm and relaxed muscles, after work.

4.8 A & B Ideally, Mark should be able to straighten his leg farther back, but you never want to force a stretch. In A, I have pulled his leg back until reaching a slight tension so that is where I stopped on this day. Just like humans, horses can be more stiff or flexible depending upon the day and how they've worked that week. I should have a deeper bend in my knees and a straighter back when asking for this stretch, as I do in B, where I'm resting the weight of Mark's leg on my knee for extra support.

WHEN

Repeat 3–7 days a week, after work.

Common Issues and Precautions

- If this is uncomfortable for you, pick your horse's hoof up and support the leg as you slowly turn and face the horse's front end before pulling back, holding either the fetlock or cannon bone for a better grip.

WHAT

In this supported stretch, you will hold your horse's hind leg while stretching it forward and up toward the belly. This is considered a _protraction_ stretch because the limb is being pulled forward.

WHY

- Stretches the _hamstrings_ and _gluteals_.

- Releases tension in the back and pelvis.

- Increases freedom of the hind end and stride length.

HOW

1 Stand next to your horse's hind leg, facing back, and ask for the foot as if you are picking the hoof.

2 Place both hands on the fetlock to support the joint.

3 Keep your knees bent as you slowly walk back toward the horse's head, stretching the leg forward and toward the front foot until you feel a slight amount of resistance.

4 After a few seconds and when the horse is comfortable, slowly begin to straighten your legs, raising the horse's leg up toward the belly. Ideally, the cannon bone is lifted parallel to the ground.

5 Hold for 10–20 seconds.

tips **for Hind Leg Reach Forward**

➤ This stretch is best with warm and relaxed muscles, after work.

➤ Allow your horse to get used to the idea of stretching slowly at first. Do not expect to reach full range the first few attempts at this exercise.

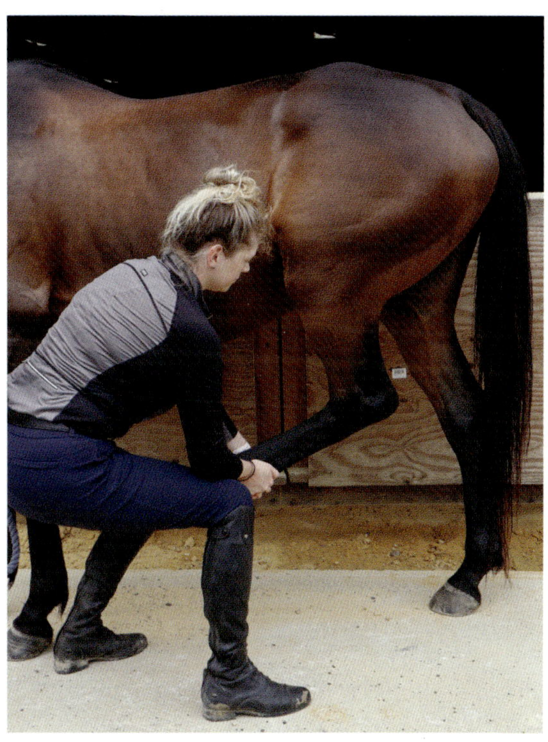

4.9 A I make sure to keep my back straight and bend my knees as I support Mark's fetlock with both hands.

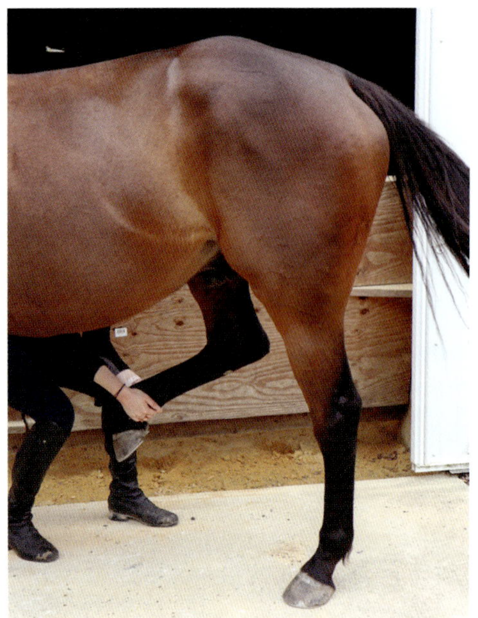

4.9 B Mark's left hind leg works to stabilize as I mobilize the right hip. Here, I've rested my elbows on my thigh to support his weight as I assist his stretch.

6 Bend your knees and lower the horse's leg before walking back and replacing the hoof gently on the ground.

7 Repeat for the same amount of time on each side (figs. 4.9 A & B).

WHEN

Repeat 3–7 days a week, after work.

Common Issues and Precautions

- Your horse may pull his leg away from your hands. Be prepared with bent knees, a straight spine and your feet out of the way.

- Cross-ties are not advisable for this stretch as your horse may need to use his head to find balance.

Front Leg Reach Forward

tips for Front Leg Reach Forward

➤ Make sure your horse's leg is stretched straight forward and not adducted or abducted toward or away from the horse's midline.

➤ Don't forget to stretch both sides, even if one is tighter than the other.

WHAT

In this *protraction* stretch, you will support your horse's front leg while stretching it forward in a straight line away from the body.

WHY

- Stretches the muscles around the shoulder, chest, front end, and back including the *latissimus dorsi, triceps, deltoid, deep pectorals, thoracic trapezius*, and *latissimus dorsi*.

- Reduces muscle stiffness in the front end stabilizers, increases range of motion, and allows for better freedom and engagement of the thoracic sling.

HOW

1. Stand beside your horse's shoulder, facing the hind end.

2. Lift your horse's leg as if picking the hoof. Switch both hands to hold the upper arm.

3. Slowly walk backward with bent knees to lengthen the leg forward until you feel a gentle resistance. Do not overstretch.

4. Once the leg is stretched forward, slowly begin to straighten your knees, allowing the leg to rise up. Optimal position is your horse's upper leg parallel to the ground with the cannon bone dangling down, however, this may not happen when first stretching in this way.

5. When your horse is comfortable with this stretch, place your outside hand on the fetlock for support and begin to straighten the lower leg forward.

6. Hold the end range of this stretch 15–30 seconds before gently releasing the leg down.

7. Repeat for the same amount of time on each side (figs. 4. 10 A & B).

WHEN

Repeat 3–7 days a week, after work.

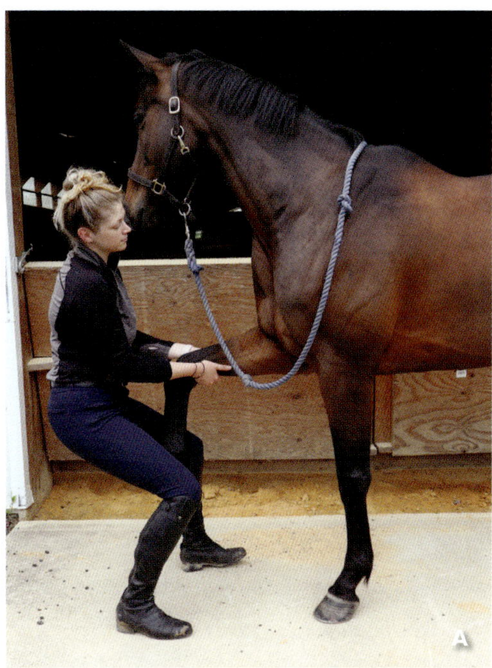

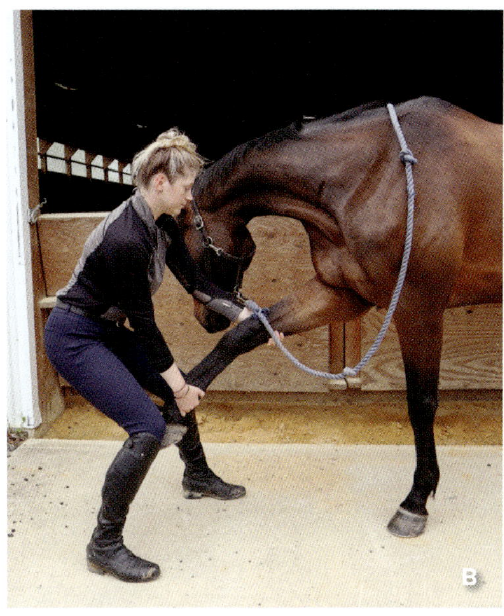

4.10 A & B I keep my back straight and knees bent to pull Mark's leg forward, before slowly straightening my legs just enough to bring his upper leg parallel to the ground (A). I make sure to support Mark's joints as I straighten his leg (B). Ideally, Mark's head is straight; however, it's more important to support the joints with my hands than bring his head back.

- Allow your horse to get used to the idea of stretching slowly at first. Do not expect to reach full range the first few attempts at this exercise.

- If your horse can easily extend his leg above parallel to ground, this stretch is not necessary and can be contraindicated as he may be overly mobile in this area.

- Your horse may pull his leg away from your hands—be prepared with bent knees, a straight spine, and your feet out of the way.

- Avoid this stretch if your horse has an acute shoulder injury or poor balance.

Front Leg Reach Back

WHAT

This retraction stretch involves supporting the horse's front leg while pulling it back toward the hind leg in order to stretch the muscles of the forehand.

WHY

Stretches the muscles of the forehand essential for bringing the limbs forward including the *cervical trapezius, omotransversarius,* and the *pectorals*.

HOW

1 Stand beside your horse's shoulder, facing the hind.

2 Lift your horse's leg as if picking the hoof.

3 Turn to face the front end, placing one hand under the fetlock and the other just above the knee for support. The knee should be bent at roughly 90 degrees.

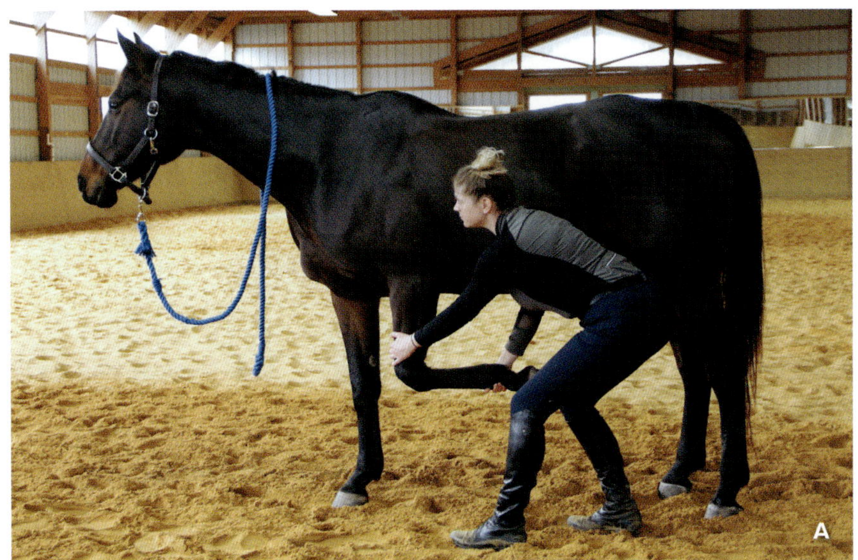

4.11 A & B I support Mark's fetlock with my right hand while my left hand gently guides the leg back from above the knee (A). I keep an eye on Mark's demeanor in case I need to release the stretch or move away quickly. I take care to pull the leg straight back, in alignment with the shoulder (B).

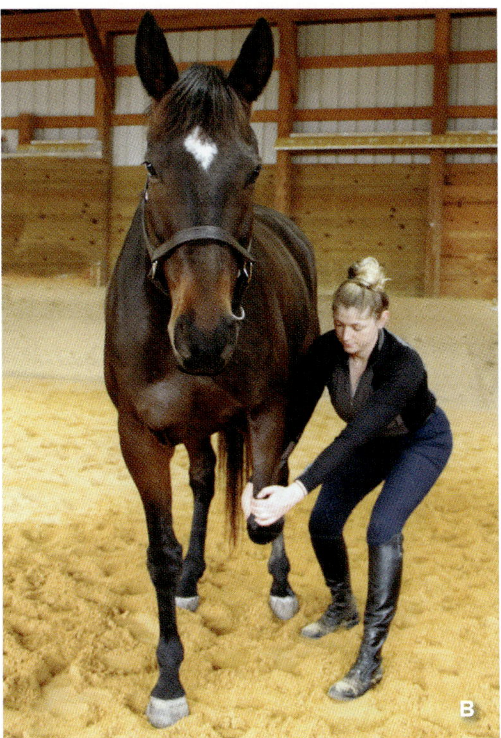

tips for Front Leg Reach Back

➤ Make sure your horse's leg is stretched straight back and not adducted or abducted toward or away from his midline.

➤ Always stretch both sides.

➤ Do not confuse this stretch with The Masterson Method® shoulder release. In that exercise, you hold at the knee and fetlock and simply allow the horse to release tension into your support. You then slowly place the foot back and down so the shoulder can release. While also a helpful exercise, it is more of a release than a stretch.

4 Begin to pull the leg back with the hand above your horse's knee until a slight resistance is met. This is a small movement.

5 Bring the leg forward again to release the stretch before placing the hoof back on the ground.

6 Repeat for the same amount of time on each side (figs. 4.11 A & B).

WHEN
This stretch can be used 3–7 days a week, after work.

Common Issues and Precautions

- Allow your horse to get used to the idea of stretching slowly at first. Do not expect to reach full range the first few attempts at this exercise.

- Your horse may pull his leg away from your hands; be prepared with bent knees, a straight spine, and your feet out of the way.

- Avoid this stretch if the horse has an acute shoulder injury or poor balance.

Dynamic Mobilization Stretches

WHAT

Dynamic mobilization stretches are active movements where the joint and muscles go through a full range of motion to increase flexibility and/or release tension. These stretches can also be considered "massage with movement."

WHY

- Small, controlled mobilization of joints and soft tissue helps heal the body.

- Can provide tension relief.

- Increases range of motion and freedom in movement.

TOOLS

- Halter and lead rope.

- A friend can be helpful to hold your horse if stall space is limited.

WHEN

Can be done every day before or after work.

tips **for Dynamic Mobilization Stretches**

➤ Beneficial to include in your warm-up.

➤ Stand close to your horse and out of kicking range.

➤ Do not try these stretches in an enclosed space like a wash stall; make sure there is room to step away if your horse loses balance or acts out.

WHAT

Mobilization of the tail in small circles, in both directions.

WHY

- Relaxes the back muscles, especially the *longissimus dorsi*.
- Helps loosen the spine.

HOW

1 Stand behind your horse and gently place your hands on his hind end, letting him know you're there.

2 Gently lift the dock of the tail until it's lined up with the spine or slightly below it.

3 Hold the tail until your horse releases tension/clamping.

4 Slowly begin to turn the tail clockwise in small circles, roughly 4 inches in diameter or the size of an apple.

5 Reverse direction (figs. 4.12 A & B).

WHEN

Every day, before or after work. Circle 3–4 times, repeating 2–3 times each direction.

4.12 A Like Tail Pull (p. 67), it's important to slowly lift the tail by the dock and allow your horse time to release any tension he may be holding.

4.12 B Tail Circles should be very small—think roughly the size of an apple.

Common Issues and Precautions

- If your horse refuses to unclamp his tail, try placing two or three fingers where the dock meets the body and press down gently. If that doesn't work, only raise the tail halfway and spend time massaging the dock with the pads of your fingers.

- If you still cannot get your horse to release his tail, move on to the **Lacrosse Ball Release** (p. 172), and if the tail is still tense, this may be an indication that a chiropractor or veterinarian should look at your horse.

- Take note of how your horse holds his tail. If the tail is held to one side, this could be an indication that the muscles are tighter on that side.

WHAT

A gentle shake and/or small circles of the hind leg to release tension in the hip.

WHY

- Releases tension in the pelvis and sacroiliac region.
- Relaxes the stifle.
- Stretches the *gluteals, bicep femoris, semimembranosus, semitendinosus, gastrocnemius,* and *deep digital flexor tendon.*

4.13 A & B Keep your horse's leg lower to the ground than in Hind Leg Reach Forward (p. 71) to keep the muscles loose (A). Support the fetlock with your hands and keep your knees bent to protect your back (B).

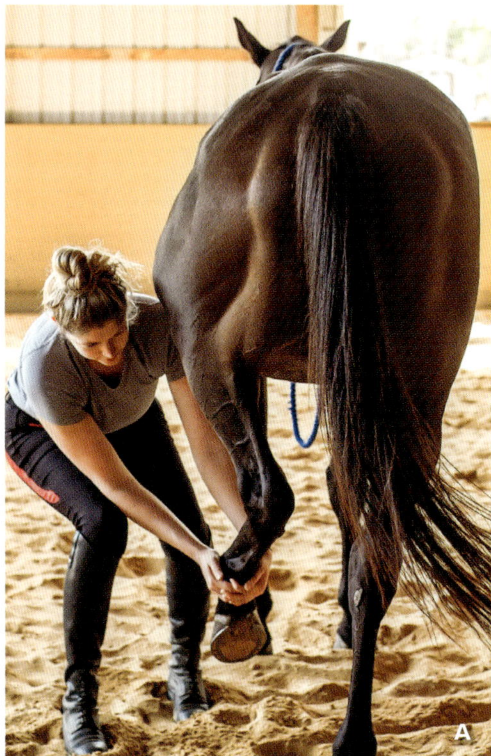

- Great stretch for horses that swap leads, have difficulty with leads in one direction, or have a short stride.

HOW

1 Stand beside your horse's back leg and ask for his foot as if you're going to pick the hoof.

2 Support the leg by placing your hands either on the end of the toe, or under the fetlock.

3 Very slowly walk toward the head, bringing the leg slightly forward, under the stifle. Stop before you reach tension.

4 Support the weight of the leg and let your horse's pelvis release down.

5 Very slowly and gently rock the leg side to side, 2–4 inches maximum.

6 Add small, baseball-sized circles 2–3 times in each direction for more mobility.

7 Repeat on the opposite side (figs. 4.13 A & B).

WHEN

Every day, before or after work, 10–20 seconds of rocking and/or 3–4 circles, repeated 2–3 times in each direction.

Common Issues and Precautions

- If your horse tries to yank his foot away, try simply holding the leg up and forward at first, allowing him to release into your hand. You may also have to hold the horse's leg slightly outside his body if he is extra tight in the hind.

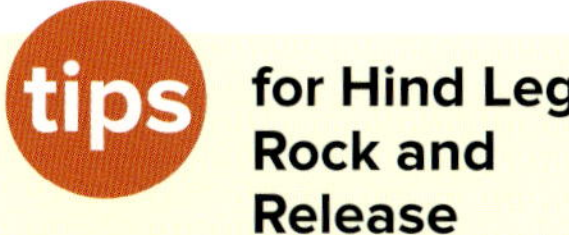

> Make sure your feet are out of the way in case your horse suddenly pulls his hoof back.

> After stretching, slowly place the foot back down and allow the horse to rest on his toe for as long as he likes for further release of the pelvis.

> Bend at your knees, not your back. You can rest your arms/ elbows on your thigh for support.

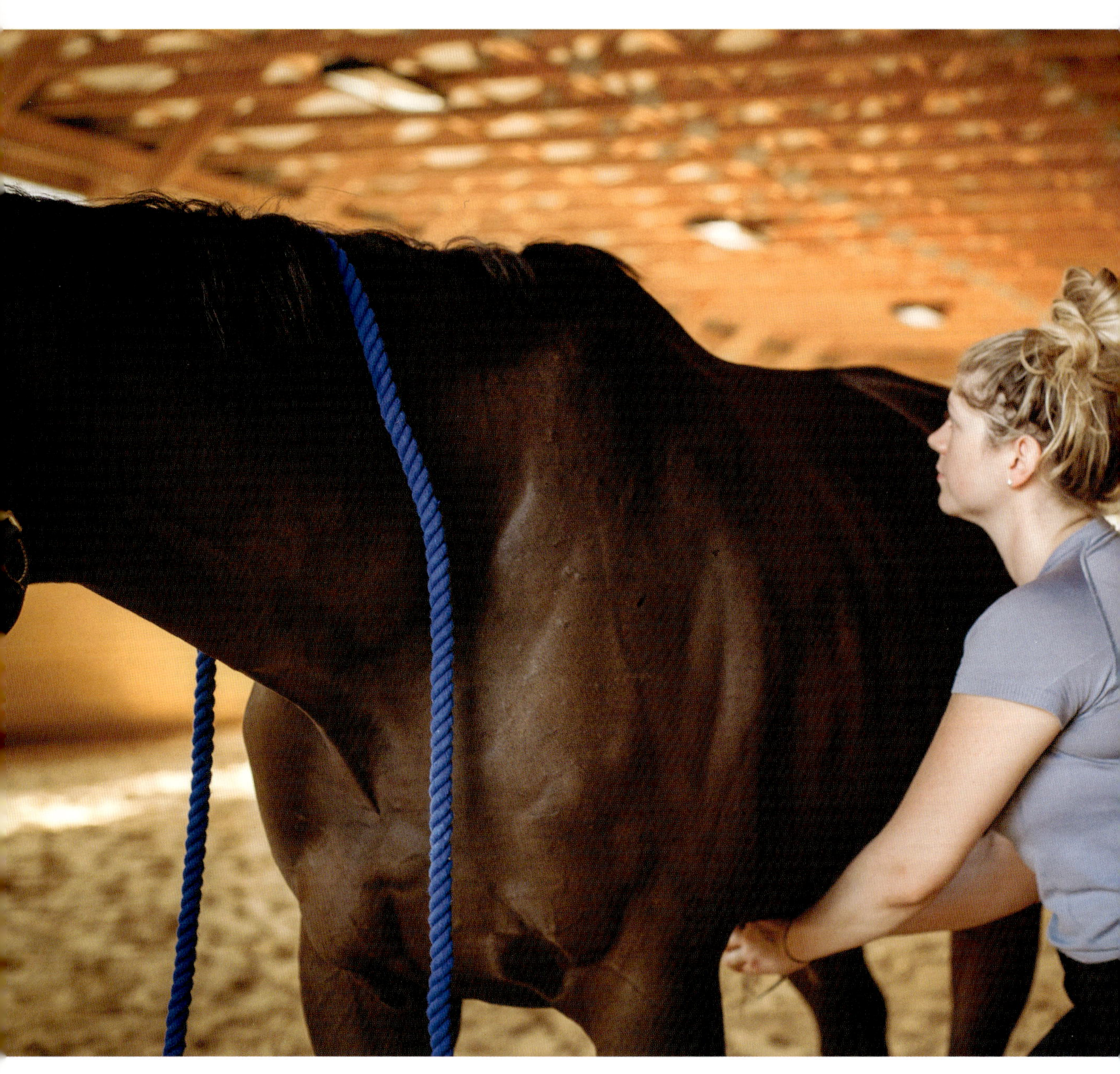

chapter 5

Core Work

In-hand core work is a great way to strengthen your horse's trunk—both topline and *abdominals*—without the weight of a rider. This is indispensable work for horses with back soreness issues or those needing to strengthen the topline without being ridden, but also for healthy horses as supplemental strengthening work. You can do these exercises before or after riding, or on rest days.

WHAT

While the majority of the exercises in this book benefit the horse's core in some way, these exercises specifically target the abdominal muscles for strengthening.

5.1 If you only have time for a handful of exercises, Cat Stretch (p. 89) should be at the top of the list for core engagement and back release.

WHY

- The core is essential as a bridge between the front and hind end. It must be strong and supple so energy can move efficiently through the body and balance can be maintained.

- A strong core is one of the most important factors for a pain-free back.

TOOLS

- Rubber-coated hoof pick.

tips for Core Work

➤ Beneficial to include in your warm-up.

➤ Stand close to the horse and out of kicking range.

➤ Do not try stretches in an enclosed space like a wash stall—make sure there is room to step away if your horse loses balance or acts out.

- Small treats low in artificial sugar that can be wrapped in the hand.

- Clicker if the horse becomes nippy.

WHEN

Can be done every day before or after work.

Nose Forward Reach

WHAT

Also considered an *incentive stretch* (see p. 55), this exercise emphasizes core engagement by asking your horse to shift his weight forward toward a treat, without moving his feet.

WHY

- Activates the thoracic sling including the *serratus ventralis, pectorals*, and *subclavius* as well as hip/pelvis stabilizers including the *gluteals, sacrocaudalis dorsalis, tensor fasciae latae, quadriceps, bicep femoris, adductors*, and *sartorius*.

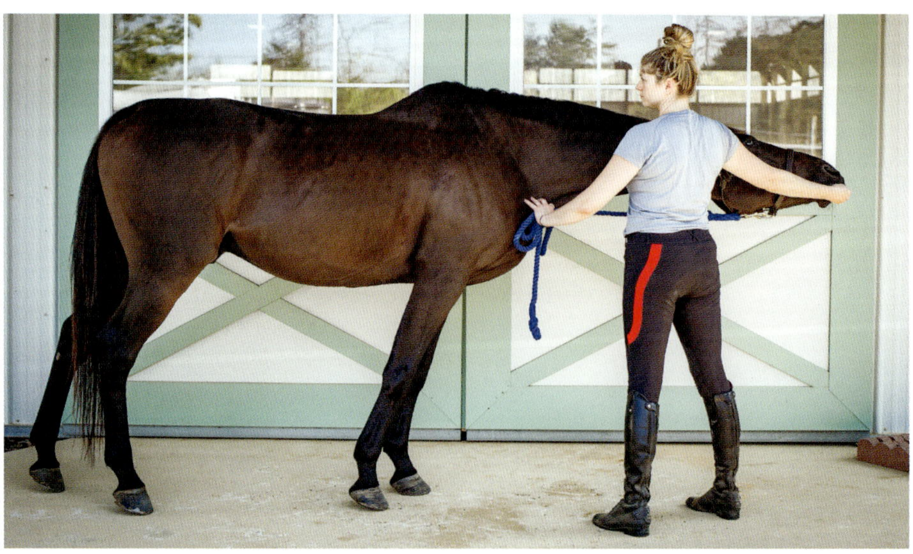

5.2 You can see Mark shifting his weight forward in order to reach the treat in front of him. Not only is he engaging his core muscles, he is stretching the neck forward, allowing for some extension and release of the underside of the neck.

- Stretches the *rectus capitis dorsalis* and *lateralis, multifidus cervicis, rhomboids, splenius,* and *trapezius.*

- Increases balance and stability.

- Improves self-carriage.

HOW

1 Stand in front of your horse and hold one hand gently against his chest to stop any forward steps.

2 Offer a treat right in front of his nose to get his attention.

3 Slowly move the treat in a straight line away from the horse, enticing him to shift his weight forward toward the treat without taking a step.

4 When using a clicker, activate it 3–4 feet in front of the horse's nose.

5 Make sure your horse's neck is straight with no tilt and the nose is pointing forward toward the incentive.

6 Hold for 10 seconds to start, working up to 30 seconds over the course of several weeks.

7 Repeat 2–4 times (fig. 5.2).

WHEN

Every day, before or after work. Hold for 10–30 seconds and repeat 2–4 times.

Common Issues and Precautions

- Don't allow your horse to raise his head too high in extension or tilt his head trying to artificially reach farther forward.

- If your horse steps forward, try being slower with the movement of the treat, ask for less reach, or do this exercise over the top of a closed door to block forward movement.

tips **for Nose Forward Reach**

➤ The goal is for your horse to shift his weight forward without actually stepping forward.

➤ Watch your feet. Your horse will most likely take a few steps before you figure out how far you can move the incentive away or how much pressure you need to keep on the chest.

➤ Use a treat that you can wrap your hand around so the horse can smell but not eat it immediately, and will hold his forward stretch.

➤ If your horse becomes nippy, especially when not asking for the stretch, spend some time training him to respond to a clicker.

➤ Allow your horse to be in control of the stretch—do not pull him into position or hold his nose down.

tips **for Weight Shift Back**

➤ The quick release is essential to keep your horse from actually stepping back.

➤ For increased difficulty, lift one of your horse's front legs and hold it up while asking for the weight shift.

WHAT

Ask your horse to shift his weight and/or rock backward without stepping back.

WHY

- Contracts the thoracic sling, *multifidus*, and muscles surrounding the stifle.

- Teaches your horse to load and engage the hind end.

HOW

1 Apply gentle pressure to your horse's lead rope or chest, asking him to shift his weight backward without moving his feet.

2 Release pressure quickly so your horse doesn't step back (fig. 5.3).

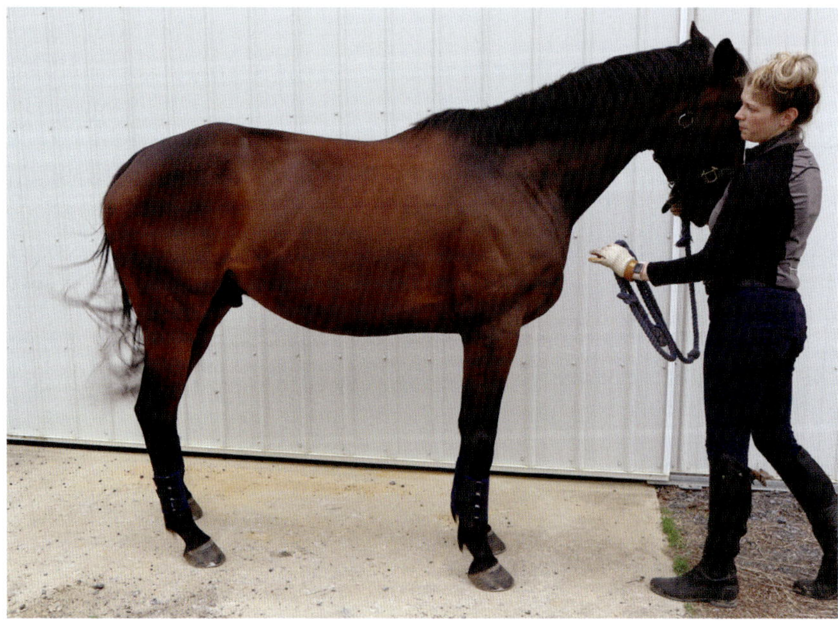

5.3 Mark has shifted his weight back onto his haunches, and his back legs are under him and engaged. Ideally, his head would stay lower than shown here, but this is a work in progress.

WHEN

Every day, before or after work. Repeat 2–4 times.

Common Issues and Precautions

- If your horse refuses to shift his weight, try lifting and holding a front leg for 10 seconds to release some of the weight on the forehand before replacing the foot and trying the exercise again.

- Placing stability pads under the front legs can also help release weight and tension in the front, activating the stabilizer muscles so they are easier to recruit. Try placing a pad under one or both front feet for 15–20 seconds before removing them and trying the exercise again.

Tail Pull Side

WHAT

By pulling your horse's tail back and to the side, he must stabilize against the pressure, engaging the hind end and increasing strength and balance.

WHY

- Activates the pelvic stabilizers including the *gluteals, bicep femoris,* and *tensor fascia latae.*
- Strengthens the stifles.
- Encourages better balance.

HOW

1 Stand 2–3 feet behind your horse and pick up his tail, ideally somewhere around halfway down the tail.

2 Begin by pulling straight back to release any compression. Relax the pressure and take a few steps to the side of your horse.

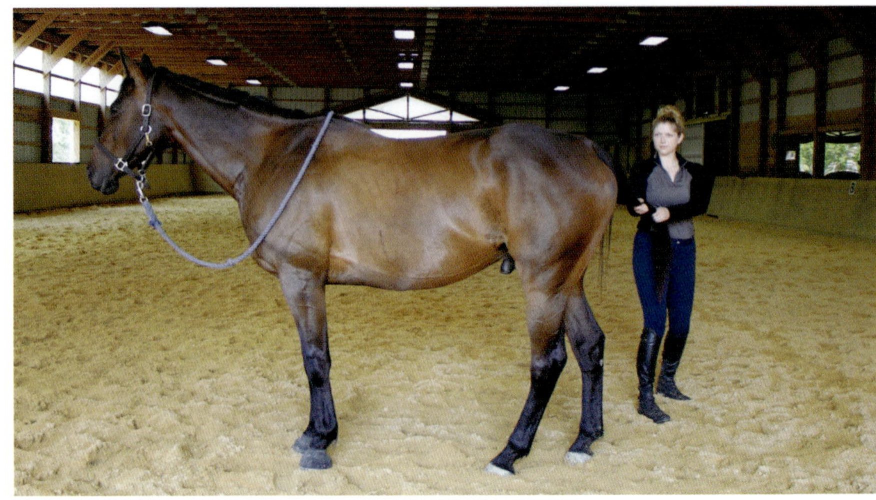

5.4 I pull just enough to see an engagement in Mark's muscles, then hold for a few seconds and release.

3 Pull the tail sideways with just enough pressure that your horse shifts his weight away from you. You should see a small activation in the *gluteal* muscles.

4 Think of the tail as an extension of the spine and don't pull too hard, higher than the croup, or at an angle less than 90 degrees to the side of the horse.

5 Hold for 5–10 seconds before releasing.

6 Repeat 5–10 times each side (fig. 5.4).

WHEN
Every day, before or after work.

Common Issues and Precautions

• Do not release the tail pressure too quickly.

• Using cross-ties is not recommended. This exercise is best done in a stall or an enclosed but large space.

WHAT

Place upward pressure at the girth line, directly under your horse's withers, slowly moving back toward the belly with continuous upward pressure. Your horse should pull his *abdominals* up and away from the contact, engaging his core, and rounding/stretching his back. This is also known as a "belly lift."

WHY

- One of the best core and topline strengthening exercises along with **Bridging** (p. 91).

- Strengthens the muscles that lift and round the back and stabilize the forehand.

- Stretches the *trapezius, longissimus dorsi, latissimus dorsi,* and the *intercostals.*

HOW

1 Stand next to your horse by his elbow with your shoulders square to his side.

2 Bend your knees if needed and place your fingers or a non-sharp object like the handle of a rubber-coated hoof pick straight up against the middle of your horse's sternum (just behind the middle of the front legs).

3 Slowly slide your hand back toward your horse's belly with continuous upward pressure, stopping right around where the back of the saddle might rest on the horse's topline, or where the ribs end.

4 Your horse should respond by lifting through his withers and then through the thoracic area as you move back.

5 Move slowly. Repeat 2–3 times before coming back to the exercise from the other side and repeating (figs. 5.5 A–C).

tips **for Cat Stretch**

➤ Slower is better in order to get your horse to hold the lift.

➤ Having the horse in a square stance is ideal but not necessary.

➤ A rounded-edge tool such as a rubber-coated hoof pick can be useful to create a bigger reaction and stretch.

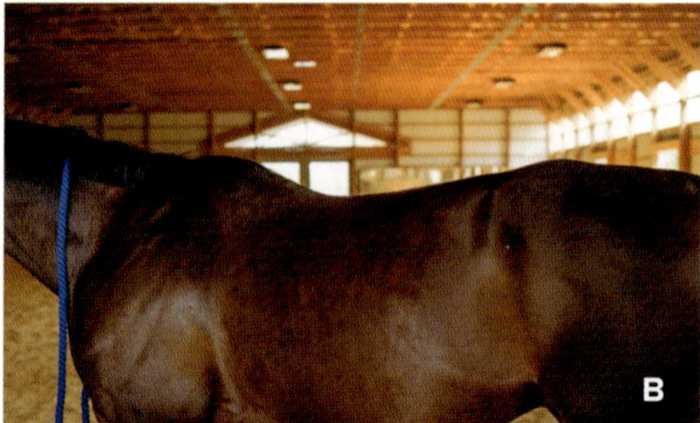

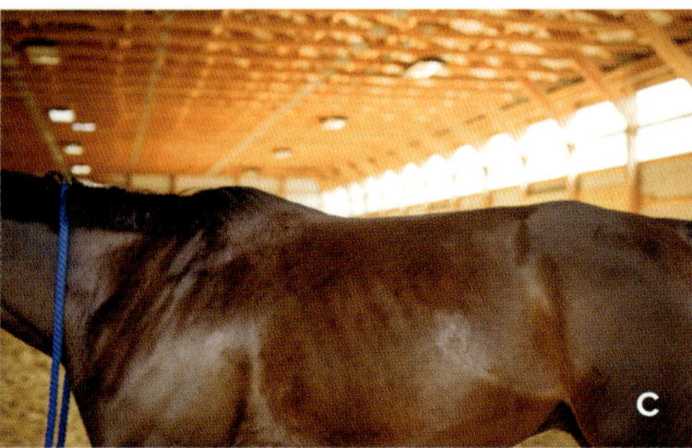

5.5 A–C I use the rubber end of a hoof pick for this exercise, pressing directly up from right below the withers to start (A). I keep my knees bent and my eyes on my horse's demeanor to assess how much pressure is needed. You can see Mark's back lift and stretch in response to the upward pressure I apply, from its original position (B) to its position with pressure (C).

WHEN

Every day, before or after work.

Common Issues and Precautions

- When you are too aggressive with pressure your horse may kick at his belly or have a "fight or flight" response to the cue instead of lifting up.

- This exercise is not recommended for horses with ulcers or who act "girthy," as this may be a stressful exercise for them and create resistance.

- If your horse becomes unreactive, try another tool. Don't use anything that can break the skin or cause pain.

- Be careful when using a treat to reinforce this work; horses may lose concentration and start turning their head in search of food while you are trying to get them to stand still.

<h1 style="text-align:center">*Bridging*</h1>

WHAT

Use your knuckles, fingertips, or a tool such as two pen caps against the top of your horse's gluteals to encourage him to tuck his pelvis away from the pressure. This will stretch your horse's back and engage his core, and is also sometimes referred to as a "butt tuck."

WHY

- One of the best core and topline strengthening exercises along with **Cat Stretch** (p. 89).

- Your horse's pelvis should rotate/tuck under, which flexes and lifts the lumbar and sacral joints also known as the low back area.

- Stabilizes the hindquarters, strengthens the abs and upper thigh muscles, and can activate the shoulder girdle if your horse also shifts his weight forward.

- Increases awareness within the nervous system from tail to head.

HOW

There are several ways to activate this exercise. Here is what I have found to be most effective:

1 Carefully stand behind your horse and pet his rump so he knows you are there.

2 Place your knuckles against your horse's glutes on either side of the tail, roughly 1–2 inches higher than the start of the tail.

3 Begin rubbing slowly in short side-to-side motions with medium pressure, and then more vigorously until the pelvis responds and tucks under. Continue for 10 seconds and then release pressure.

4 Repeat two times before coming back to the exercise later (figs. 5.6 A–C).

> ➤ Each horse reacts differently so you may have to play with pressure and direction, but the goal is the same: to get a slow and gradual tuck of the pelvis and stretch of the lumbar spine. Starting with fast and firm pressure can cause too quick and intense a reaction.

> ➤ Slower is better in order to keep your horse from jerking into a reaction or kicking out.

> ➤ A square stance for your horse is ideal but not necessary.

> ➤ Gloves can be helpful to protect your knuckles, but they may get dirty.

5.6 A–C Comparing photos A and B, you can see the significant tuck Mark does with his pelvis when pressure is applied by my knuckles. His back is stretching, and his gluteals and abs are engaged. Some horses respond better to pressure a little higher up, so it may take some trial and error to find a "trigger point" for your horse. Mark is sensitive and responds to both my knuckles and my fingernails against his hindquarters (C).

Variation 1

Alternatively, you can try using your fingernails or two pen caps to trigger bridging by placing downward pressure starting on either side of the sacrum. Draw a large arc with both hands down and away from each other toward the hips.

Variation 2

If your horse does not respond, stand to the side of his hip and place your fingers on either side of the spine starting at the tail. Use gentle downward or pinching pressure and slowly work forward, away from the tail.

WHEN

Every day, before or after work.

Common Issues and Precautions

- If you are too aggressive with pressure, the horse may kick or have a "fight or flight" response to the cue instead of tucking under.

- If you are worried that your horse may kick out, try doing this over a closed stall door for protection.

- If your horse becomes unreactive, try using a different method. I find that with practice, my horse has become more reactive to my cues.

- Be careful when using a treat to reinforce this work; horses may lose concentration and start turning their head in search of food while you are trying to get them to stand still.

chapter 6

In-Hand Strengthening Work

In-hand strengthening work, like core work, is an essential tool for both healthy horses and those that need conditioning without the weight, imbalances, or potentially confusing cues of a rider. These exercises can increase your horse's confidence, balance, and control, while also strengthening the bond between horse and human. They are also great exercises for "active rest days."

WHAT

These in-hand exercises give you different options for training your horse from the ground.

6.1 In-hand walking over raised ground poles allows your horse to navigate his feet over obstacles without confusing signals or hand-holding from the rider. This increases, strength, agility, and confidence for the horse.

WHY

- This is a great way to include strengthening work without weight on your horse's back.

- It can be helpful to introduce/teach exercises from the ground that can later be used when riding.

- You can move poles and change exercises easily to accommodate your horse without mounting/dismounting multiple times.

TOOLS

- Longe whip

for In-Hand Strengthening Work

➤ Start with a halter and lead rope before using a bridle and bit.

- Gloves

- Ground poles, risers (pole lifts), and/or cavalletti

WHEN

Strive to do in-hand/groundwork at least twice a week. Most horses can benefit from one or two in-hand exercises at the start of every session. Keep in mind that these exercises can be just as difficult for a horse as under-saddle work, so don't overdo both in-hand and under-saddle work in the same day, and don't repeat the same exercises on back-to-back days.

The Back-Up

WHAT

Ask your horse to take several steps back, maintaining straightness. Backing up requires the front end to lift, the abs to engage, and the three major hind joints—sacrum, stifle, and hock—to flex and bear additional weight.

WHY

- This is a low-impact, core activation exercise that helps with balance, rounds the back/tucks the pelvis, and strengthens the hind end.

- Requires a lifting and, therefore, mobilization and strengthening of the *thoracic sling* and *flexor chain*. Strengthens the *nuchal ligament*, *supraspinatus* and *trapezius*.

- Stretches and lengthens the *flexor tendons* and *hamstrings*.

- Increases coordination of the body from front to back and also side to side.

- Slower gaits like the walk increase engagement of smaller muscles.

- A good precursor to the **Rein-Back** under saddle (p. 162).

- Helps develop work through the back that is essential in collection.

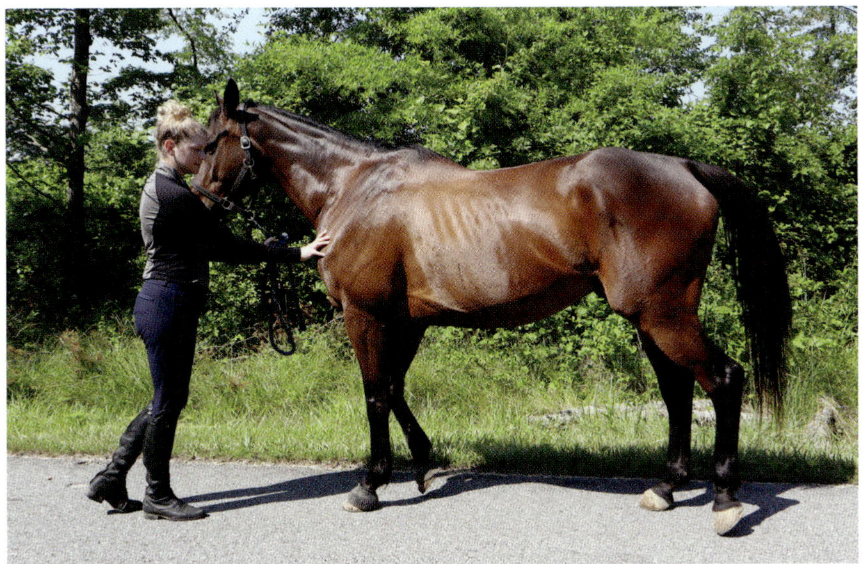

6.2 I am mostly using pressure to Mark's chest to ask him to back up, with light backward tension on the lead rope as well. I would like to see a lower head and a higher lift of the feet, which is easier to get after warming up or when backing up a slight incline. You can see him moving his feet back in diagonal pairs.

- An especially helpful exercise if there is weakness in the stifles or tightness in the hamstrings.

HOW

1 Start with a square halt.

2 Stand in front of your horse and place gentle pressure on the lead rope or reins toward the horse's body. Make sure to use a voice command like "Back" that can also be used when riding.

3 If using a halter, you can give a gentle bump to the rope to get the horse's attention, but do not do this when using a bit.

4 It may also be helpful to place a hand against your horse's chest or shoulder to encourage the backing motion.

for the Back-Up

➤ Never ask for more than 4–5 steps at a time before walking forward as a reward.

➤ Your horse should step his feet back in diagonal pairs, like in the trot.

➤ If your horse has never backed in hand, start with a halter and lead rope before using a bit.

➤ For an advanced modification, try backing up a small hill. This can increase mobility in the *lumbosacral joint* and activate the *spinal stabilizers, pectorals,* and *thoracic sling* more intensely. This is not a good modification for horses with an arthritic back or hocks.

5 Ask the horse to take 3–4 steps straight back and then release pressure
and walk forward as a reward before repeating.

6 Walk up to 20–30 steps backward a day, but never all at once (fig. 6.2).

WHEN

Every day, before or after work, up to 30 steps. Walking to the arena can be
a good time to add a few back-up steps. Back up 4 steps, walk forward 10,
repeat.

Common Issues and Precautions

- If your horse is not walking straight back, do this exercise next to
a wall or fence. You can also stand on the side he veers toward
and put pressure on that shoulder with your hand, or ask for fewer
steps at a time.

- Your horse should drop his head but not curl too deeply into the
chest, which is an evasion tactic.

- If your horse is shuffling instead of lifting the back feet, try this
exercise on a harder surface like pavement to jumpstart the nervous system. This may also be an indication that your horse needs
to activate the hind end before being able to properly back up. Try
Criss-Cross In-Hand (p. 101) and then come back to this exercise.
You can also hold a whip and tap the legs gently to encourage a
higher lift.

- Never use the **Back-Up** as punishment.

Varied Surface Walk

WHAT

Walking on different surfaces including asphalt, grass, hard-packed dirt, sand, and water can build ligament and tendon strength and increase proprioception.

WHY

* Awakens the horse's nervous system and increases proprioception.

* Asphalt and hard-packed ground can tighten ligaments and tendons in the lower leg—essential for support since there are no muscles below the knee.

* Deeper footing or water can add up to 50 percent more work. This means it can potentially be useful in strengthening the stifles, but there is also a higher risk of injury when done incorrectly.

* It's helpful to train in different footing within the controlled environment of your home farm before introducing these elements at a horse show or on a long trail ride.

* Walking is best for hard surfaces to avoid excessive concussion whereas trotting is the best gait for deep sand—the hind end is more likely to trail out in the walk and canter and cause problems.

HOW

1 Find a flat, hard surface to begin. This can mean detouring over the parking lot on the way to the barn every few days, or hand walking on trails.

2 Hand walking is the best way to start this strengthening work. Riding on hard surfaces is the next progression, but this should be taken slowly so tissues have time to build and rest.

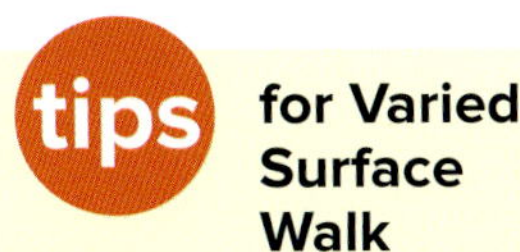

tips **for Varied Surface Walk**

➤ Err on the side of caution when working on varied surfaces. Less is more.

➤ A shallow creek is an ideal place to ride. Not only will you have the resistance of the water, but you will also be getting the anti-inflammatory benefits of cold water. Make sure there are no hazards in the water before proceeding with your horse.

3 If your horse feels tired or sluggish while working in deep or compacted sand, rest. Tears can occur when a horse is forced to work in this footing for too long (fig. 6.3).

WHEN

Start with 10 minutes of active walking on varied surfaces every 3–4 days. Slowly increase to 20 minutes up to 3 days a week, but never on consecutive days.

Common Issues and Precautions

- Shoes are essential for horses you plan to ride on asphalt to protect their feet and avoid slipping.

- Be careful when working in deep sand. Think about how tiring walking on the beach can be, and aim for footing similar to the wet part of beach sand, close to the water.

- Deep footing can be dangerous. Try walking around in the footing for a few minutes by yourself to see how much effort it takes to lift your own legs before working your horse on the surface.

Criss-Cross In-Hand

WHAT

This exercise involves walking your horse in tight circles, resulting in a lateral yielding or crossing of the horse's hindquarters. This is similar to **Turn on the Forehand** (p. 144) but with continued forward motion and can also be known as "disengaging the hindquarters."

WHY

- Increases strength, coordination, and suppleness across the body.

- Creates dynamic flexibility through the rib cage and loin (the area between the last rib and croup, and also the pivot point of the horse's back).

- Strengthens the *adductors* and other muscles surrounding the pelvis as the inside leg steps up under the belly.

- Creates mobility in the scapula.

- Asking for a bend will stretch and strengthen the *oblique* muscles that flex and stabilize the trunk, support the topline and strengthen the muscles involved in lifting the back, also known as the core (*multifidi, abs, iliopsoas*).

- A good starting point for turn on the forehand.

- Think of this as an *oblique* crunch. It's a good exercise for improving gait irregularities, falling in/out, and stiffness in the bend.

HOW

1 Start by leading your horse in a small circle roughly 10 meters wide, holding a long whip.

2 Ask for a small inside bend on the circle.

3 Begin to close the circle, moving slightly back toward the horse's hindquarters and angling the whip toward his back legs.

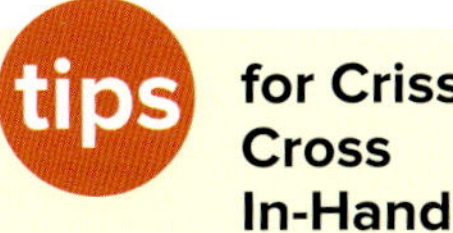

tips **for Criss-Cross In-Hand**

- ➤ Try to maintain a consistent tempo.

- ➤ Start with 3–4 steps and then walk forward. Never do more than one full revolution at a time, this can strain the stifle and cause *glute* and low-back soreness.

- ➤ A dressage or longe whip is helpful for this, as well as boots or wraps to protect the horse's legs from hitting each other.

6.4 A & B I'm holding a longe whip and asking Mark to walk a tight circle around me. His inside hind leg reaches forward and across the outside hind leg but his pelvis stays relatively level (A). Make sure to repeat the work in both directions (B). Some horses respond better if you lead them in a small circle rather than try to do a small longe circle.

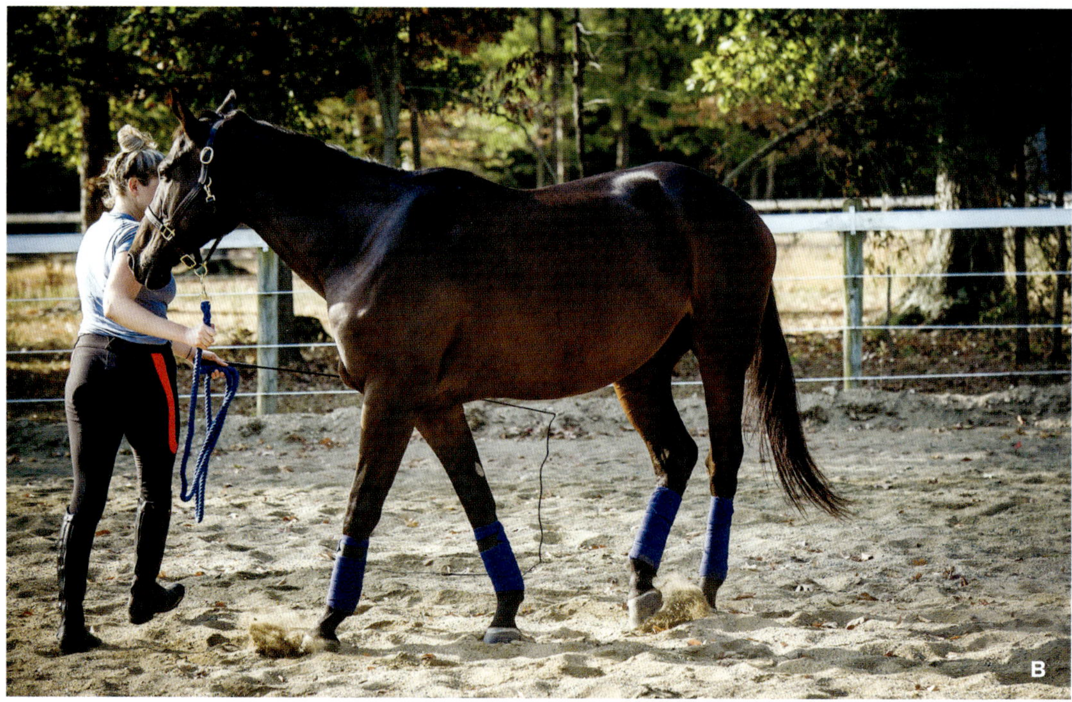

4 Your horse should tighten the circle, crossing his inside hind leg under-neath himself and in front of his outside hind leg as he moves around you. If the horse crosses his inside hind leg behind the outside hind or hits the outside leg with his inside hoof, make your circle slightly larger.

5 Ask for 3–4 cross steps before walking straight forward, working up to a complete circle.

6 You can either continue walking with the horse as you ask for the lateral movement, or stop and ask for an extra small longe circle around you.

7 Change directions and repeat.

8 Continuous forward motion of the horse is key to encourage gradual suppleness (figs. 6.4 A & B).

WHEN

This is a useful tool for warming up, finishing a longe session, or whenever doing in-hand work.

Common Issues and Precautions

- Your horse's hind legs should ideally cross without the inside hip dropping—this is a compensation. Try stretching the hind legs to help disengage the pelvis if your horse is dropping, then work on fewer repetitions and add hill work and **The Back-Up** (p. 96) to your program.

- Make sure not to exaggerate the inside bend.

WHAT

Walk over 2–6 ground poles spaced 2 1/2–3 feet apart with an even, active tempo. After several successful repetitions, raise alternate sides of each pole, walking over the center. Progress to walking over poles with both sides raised.

WHY

tips **for Walking Ground Pole Progressions**

➤ Your horse's tail should swing as his trunk swings.

- Increases pelvic stability, which, in turn, allows the horse to transfer weight off the forehand and onto the haunches.

- Engages the thoracic sling, lifting the trunk between the scapula.

- Helps recruit the *multifidus* muscle, which supports the back.

- Creates symmetry and balance within the body.

- Increases flexion of the joints in the legs and hips.

HOW

1 Hold your horse's lead rope loosely in order to allow him to navigate the poles with a free head and neck.

6.5 A–C First, we start with simple ground poles **(A)**. Next, we progress to ground poles lifted on alternating sides, aiming for the middle **(B)**. We finish with both sides of the ground poles lifted, requiring the most coordination and bend in the joints. **(C)**.

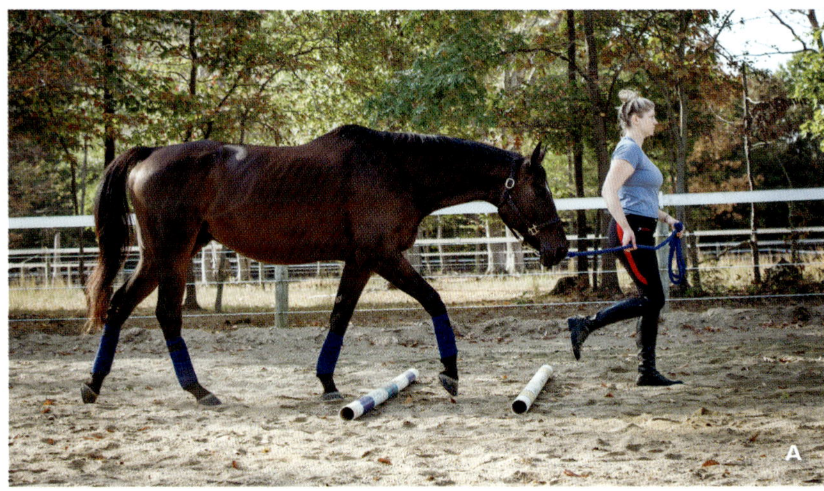

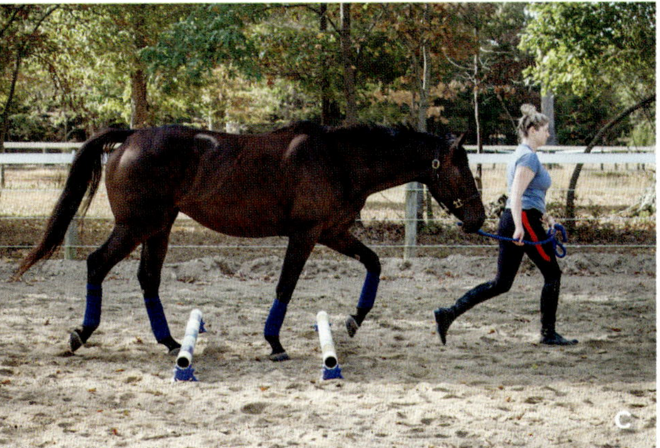

2 Start with two poles on the ground and add more after your horse has shown the ability to lift his limbs actively upward and stay calm and balanced.

3 Progress by either adding more poles or lifting the poles—never both at once.

4 Aim for the center of each pole (figs. 6.5 A–C).

Common Issues and Precautions

- If your horse struggles with this exercise, change the spacing of the poles to make it easier, use fewer poles, or lower the poles to the ground.

- Wrap your horse's legs or use boots to protect him from over-stepping or hitting the poles with bare legs.

- Many horses are most successful at this exercise if you lead them properly from beside their head instead of from out front. My horse is most successful "following the leader" over the poles. Experiment to see what works for you, as long as the horse doesn't speed up and you are not rushing or pulling him.

Longe Work

By itself, longeing is not a particularly useful tool for reeducating poor movement patterns. Working on a constant bend can put added stress on the joints and muscles and, when not done properly, there is no connection and the horse can become strung out. However, it is a great way to observe your horse's way of moving and muscle patterns, and using various props such as poles, body wraps, or the Equiband® can make it an invaluable part of training.

WHAT

Longing in a thoughtful and safe manner is a great option for working your horse without the weight or distraction of a rider on his back, and a good way to reinforce voice commands as well as create strength, suppleness, and balance. Longe work is not recommended for horses with stifle injuries given that the horse must work on a circle, and should be used in moderation.

7.1 Longeing with proper care and technique is a good way to diversify your training program. I try to incorporate longe work once or twice a week as an alternative to riding, and it's perfect for days I don't have time to tack up and ride. It is important to treat longe work like you would ridden work, and the longe line as if it were reins. The line should stay taut and your body and hands should be engaged and controlled. Your horse should be paying attention to your cues the entire time he is on the longe.

WHY

- Beneficial for general strength and conditioning without a rider's weight.

- Stretches the topline.

- Engages the core and hindquarters.

- Increases reaction to voice aids.

for Longe Work

➤ Change direction every 5–6 minutes.

➤ Proper longe technique is to make a triangle shape with your body (hips facing the horse), the longe line and the whip, framing the horse. Your body position should reflect your riding position: hands soft, elbows in near your sides, thumbs up, core engaged.

➤ Always start the horse on his easier side and warm up at the walk.

➤ Never wrap the longe line around your hand—fold it back and forth and feed the line out from the top.

➤ Use consistent voice commands: "Walk on," "Ter-ot," "And canter," "And whoaaaa." Raise the inflection of your voice for an upward transition and use a lower and slower tone for downward transitions.

➤ Poll, eye, and mouth of the horse should be facing slightly inward, but not cranked in.

TOOLS

● Gloves.

● Longe line—a long, single rein that is the main communication between horse and human, typically 25–35 feet long.

● Longeing cavesson—looks like a halter but typically has a padded noseband with metal rings on top. The noseband should lie on the nasal bone, roughly four fingers above the nostrils. These cavessons are typically better than a halter because they give you more control and are less likely to slip out of place.

● Surcingle—a wide band that goes around the horse like a saddle and girth. A surcingle should have metal rings at various points along the top and sides for side reins or other longeing equipment. This can be used over a saddle or in place of one.

● Longe whip—a whip that is usually 5 feet 7 inches long with a lash at the end, often around 6 feet long.

● Boots or wraps—horses have more potential to interfere or kick themselves when traveling on a circle so it is important to use leg protection, especially when longeing over poles.

● Consider using running side-reins or Vienna Reins as a tool to help your horse stretch forward and downward, seeking contact—set the length equal on both sides at first so the inside rein gives as the horse bends inward. Advance to shortening the inside rein by 2–3 holes to encourage the inside bend.

WHEN

Try to include longeing 1–3 times a week instead of riding. Keep sessions short, especially at the beginning, and aim for 20–30 minutes. Switch direction often.

WHAT

Upward and downward transitions between gaits on the longe line build both strength and responsiveness to voice commands.

WHY

- Transitions are a fundamental way to engage and strengthen the hind end and topline.

- Softens the neck.

- Increases reaction to voice aids.

- Increases balance.

- Engages the abdominals.

HOW

1 Warm up at the walk, asking for an active tempo and keeping steady contact with the longe line.

2 Ask for the trot with an upward inflection of the voice while saying "Ter-ot." Encourage with a gentle flick of the whip toward the hock without making contact.

3 After several circles, ask for the walk by lowering the tone of your voice and saying "And waaaalk." If the horse does not listen, think about relaxing your posture, give a light tug on the longe line, or try holding the whip in front of the horse

7.2 A & B There should be slightly less slack in the longe line in photo A, and my hips should be rotated to the right so that they are facing the horse. It is easy to relax when your horse is walking, but you should maintain proper longe technique at all gaits. I have better contact with the longe line in B; however, I should be folding the slack into my right hand for safety. Mark is alert and responsive to my voice commands.

 **for Longe Line Transitions**

- Be patient with the timing of the transitions. They may be slow at first—the most important thing is the quality of the new gait.

- Do not become "whip happy." If the whip is over-used, the horse will stop responding to it. Your horse should also not be afraid of the whip. If he is, spend time teaching the horse that the whip is not meant to hurt him.

- Try to maintain a consistent-sized circle to help with balance.

- Never step back from your horse. Always ask him to move away from you when maintaining the size of your circle.

- If the horse refuses to make an upward transition, shorten the longe line and move toward him briefly in order to urge him forward more effectively. Do not move toward the horse without shortening the longe line.

- Increase difficulty by adding transitions within the gait (lengthening and collecting).

- Think of the whip as an extension of the arm and use a flick of the wrist, not strength, to use it.

- Downward transitions can take more time than upward transitions. Try this progression: trot 10 steps, walk 10 steps. Trot 10 steps, walk 9 steps. Trot 10 steps, walk 8 steps. Trot 10 steps, walk 7 steps. Continue until you trot 10 steps and walk only one step (figs. 7.2 A & B).

instead of behind. Stay calm and be patient with the downward transition at first.

4 After a circle or two at the walk, ask for another upward transition using the increased inflection in the voice while saying "Ter-ot," just as before.

5 Begin to ask for more frequent transitions, every circle and then every half-circle, building up to asking for an upward transition almost immediately after the downward transition is complete.

Common Issues and Precautions

- If your horse is rushing, gently vibrate the longe line and use a calm voice to relax him.

- Your horse should keep a steady head and neck as he moves into the new gait.

- If your horse takes short, choppy strides in the new gait, encourage him with your voice and whip to move forward.

- If using side-reins, remember that they are not meant to restrict or create a fake "frame," but rather to provide contact for the horse to reach into.

- Cantering can be difficult for some horses on the longe line, so only add small amounts of this work until the horse has built up more strength.

<h1 style="text-align:center">*Spiraling*</h1>

WHAT

Spiraling involves gradually decreasing and increasing the size of your longe circle at the walk, trot or canter.

WHY

- Creates suppleness and balance.

- Small circles (10–11 meters) engage the deep *epaxial* muscles of the spine, increasing stability and drawing the scapula back. The horse is encouraged to step under and lighten the shoulder.

- Helps create space and mobility between the vertebrae.

- This is a useful exercise for horses that lean to one side and push their shoulder forward because it requires the shoulder to draw back dynamically, increasing strength and balance.

HOW

1 At the walk, trot, or canter, start on a 20-meter circle with a slight inside bend.

2 After one or two circles, begin to draw the longe line in, asking for a smaller circle around 11 meters wide.

3 Keep the circle small for one to two revolutions before pushing the horse back out over the span of 2–3 circles, maintaining the inside bend.

tips for **Spiraling**

➤ Try to maintain a consistent tempo and slight inside bend.

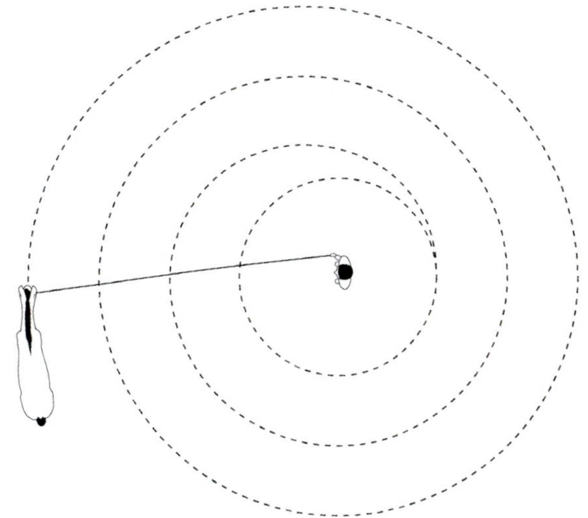

7.3 This illustration shows the path your horse should travel on for Spiraling on the longe. This exercise can also be ridden under saddle (p. 134).

4   If you have trouble sending your horse out to make the circle bigger, aim your whip at your horse's shoulder or take a step toward him. Be sure not to let the horse pull or push you completely out of your own space.

5   Keep the 20-meter circle for 2–3 revolutions before asking for another spiral (figs. 7.3 and 7.4).

Common Issues and Precautions

- If your horse drops his shoulder or dives inside, increase the size of the circle and drive him forward.

- If your horse turns and faces you, check your posture. Your hips, arms, and core are driving forces and should make a triangle with the horse's body. You should have a steady connection and avoid slack in the longe line. Always ask for forward movement.

- Never wrap the longe line around your hand or let it fall to the ground. Fold it/feed it out as needed.

Ground Poles on a Bend at the Walk

WHAT

Ask your horse to walk actively over 2–6 ground poles spaced roughly 3 feet apart in a fan or half-circle shape, on the longe line.

WHY

- Increases *core* stability, spinal mobility, and joint flexion.
- Increases side-to-side swing of the sacrum, relieving tension in the lower back.
- Stretches and flexes the *psoas*, which are important trunk stabilizers needed for collection work.
- Creates flexion of the stifle and suppleness throughout the body.
- Ground poles give sensory feedback to the horse to lift his legs, reprograming the nervous system and helping to correct gait abnormalities.

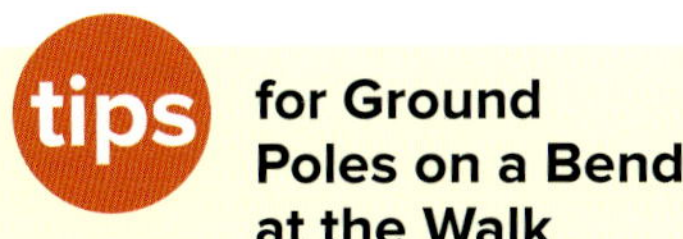

tips **for Ground Poles on a Bend at the Walk**

➤ Try to maintain a consistent tempo and slight inside bend.

➤ Encourage a long-and-low headset.

➤ Maintain steady contact with the longe line.

➤ Start with fewer poles and add more to increase difficulty.

HOW

1. Place 2–6 poles in a fan shape on a half circle, roughly 3 feet apart.

2. Start by warming your horse up at the walk and trot on a 20-meter circle, 5–10 minutes in each direction, near the poles but not over them.

3. When your horse is warm, move the longe circle toward the poles and aim your horse over the middle of each pole at the walk.

4. Repeat the exercise 4–6 times before pulling the longe circle away from the poles to give your horse a break.

5. Reverse and repeat.

6   Repeat 3–5 times.

7   Emphasize an active—but not rushing—walk (fig. 7.5).

Common Issues and Precautions

- Aim for the middle of each pole. If your horse is struggling with spacing, send him out to the farther/wider side of the poles for more room, or make your circle smaller to aim the horse toward the closer/shorter distance between each pole.

- Use leg protection, like boots or wraps.

- Don't make this monotonous and overdo it. Keep this exercise short and sweet to get the most benefit.

- If your horse is lacking strength or balance, try placing three poles in a straight line instead of on a curve and allow him to navigate the poles while going straight, turning before and after the poles to complete the longe circle.

WHAT

Ask your horse to trot evenly over 2–6 ground poles spaced roughly 4–4 1/2 feet apart (at the center) in a fan or half-circle shape, on the longe line.

WHY

- Creates flexion of the stifle and suppleness throughout the body, especially in the neck and ribs.

- The outside muscles stretch while the inside ribs and haunches contract and work.

- Trot poles improve mobility of the limbs and target the larger back muscles, engaging the *spinal stabilizers* and releasing the *extensor muscle* chain.

- Engages the *quadriceps* and increases pelvic stability.

- Engages the core.

- Helps create a clear rhythm and stride length for the horse as he navigates the poles.

- Poles give sensory feedback to the horse to lift his legs, reprograming the nervous system and helping to correct gait abnormalities.

7.6 Mark is wearing the Equiband® to awaken proprioceptors and to encourage engagement of the *abdominals* and rounding of the back as he trots over the poles.

HOW

1 Place 2–6 poles in a fan shape on a half circle, 4–4 1/2 feet apart in the middle of each pole.

2 Start by warming the horse up at the walk and trot on a 20-meter circle, 5–10 minutes in each direction, near the poles but not over them.

tips for Ground Poles on a Bend at the Trot

➤ Your job is to ask for a steady rhythm and guide your horse to the center of the poles. Your horse's job is to lift his legs and navigate over the poles.

➤ Encourage a long-and-low headset.

➤ Maintain steady contact with the longe line.

➤ Try to maintain a consistent tempo—working but not rushing—and small inside bend.

➤ Start with fewer poles and add more to increase difficulty.

➤ Try setting up ground poles at walking distance on the inside/closer track over the poles and trotting distance over the middle or outside track so you can work through both gaits.

➤ You can also set up two circles of poles near each other and move between the two to work at both the walk and trot (fig. 7.7).

➤ For an advanced exercise, pull 1–2 poles out of the pattern. The horse must then maintain the rhythm without every pole still being in place as a guide.

3 After warming up, move the longe circle toward the poles and aim your horse over the middle of each pole at the trot. Repeat the exercise 4–6 times before moving the longe circle away from poles to give your horse a rest.

4 Reverse and repeat 3–5 times (fig. 7.6).

Common Issues and Precautions

● Aim for the middle of each pole. If the horse is struggling with spacing, make the circle slightly smaller or push the circle wider to adjust.

● Use leg protection, like boots or wraps.

● Don't overdo this exercise and make it monotonous. Keep it short and sweet to get the most benefit.

● If your horse is lacking strength or balance, try placing three poles in a straight line instead of on a curve and allow him to navigate the poles while going straight, turning before and after the poles to complete the longe circle.

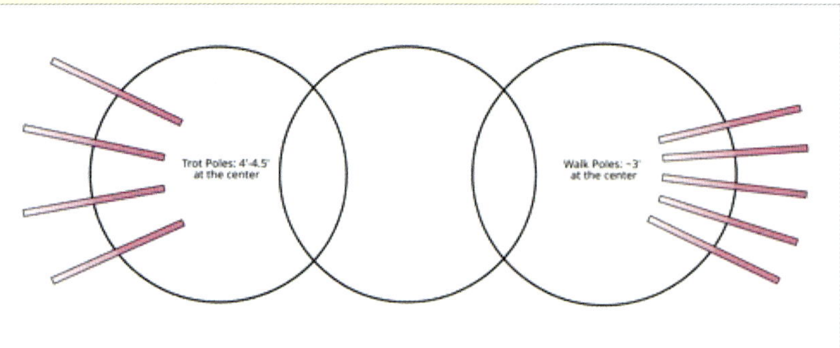

7.7 You can set up two circles with poles near each other, one with the appropriate distances for the walk and the other set up for the trot, and switch between the two in order to work at both gaits.

Ground Poles on a Bend at the Canter

WHAT

Ask your horse to canter calmly over 2–6 ground poles spaced roughly 9–12 feet apart in a fan or half-circle shape, on the longe line.

WHY

- Cantering targets the *thoracic sling*—essential for suspending the trunk between the front legs and enabling the hind end to swing and engage under the body.

- Loosens the shoulders due to the forward/back rocking motion of the canter.

- Improves both flexion/lifting and extension of the back.

- Creates a clear rhythm for the horse.

- Flexes the stifle and creates suppleness throughout the whole body.

- Poles give sensory feedback to the horse to lift his legs, reprograming the nervous system and helping to correct gait abnormalities.

HOW

1 Place 2–6 poles on a half circle roughly 9–12 feet apart at the center.

2 Start by warming the horse up at the walk, trot, and canter on a 20-meter circle, 5–10 minutes in each direction, near the poles but not over them.

3 After warming up, move the longe circle toward the poles. Pick up a solid canter with ample time to create a rhythm before aiming for the center of the poles.

4 Repeat 2–4 times before pulling the longe circle away from the poles to give the horse a break, coming back to the trot and then walking a few minutes.

tips for Ground Poles on a Bend at the Canter

➤ Encourage a long-and-low headset.

➤ Maintain steady contact with the longe line. Your horse may jump the poles the first few times so be ready.

➤ Try to maintain a consistent and relaxed but active rhythm, and a slight inside bend. If your horse does jump the poles, try to stay steady and calm. With repetition, he should eventually work over the poles without changing his stride.

➤ Start with fewer poles and add more to increase difficulty.

➤ Try setting up two half-circles of poles on either side of the arena in the shape of a Venn diagram, one with trot poles and one with canter poles. Move between the two after several repetitions to include transition work (fig. 7.8).

5 Reverse and repeat, finding a good canter each time before asking the horse to go over the poles.

6 Repeat 2–5 times.

Common Issues and Precautions

● Aim for the middle of each pole. If the horse is struggling with spacing, make the circle slightly smaller or push the circle wider to adjust.

● Canter work can be difficult for some horses on the longe line. Don't do too many repetitions in one session, and give the horse lots of rest breaks.

● If your horse is lacking strength or balance, try using 1–2 poles in a straight line instead of on a curve and allow him to navigate the poles while going straight, turning before and after the poles to complete the circle.

● You can also try placing a pole every quarter-circle for a total of 4 poles to help your horse find a consistent canter. This is also called a **Strength Circle** (p. 154).

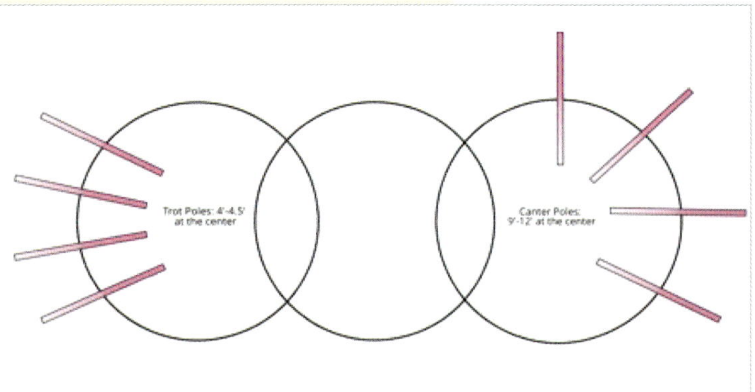

7.8 It can work well to have two half-circles of poles on either side of the arena—one with trot poles and one with canter poles—so you can move between the two and practice transitions.

Raised Ground Poles on a Bend

WHAT

Ask your horse to work over lifted ground poles or cavalletti on the longe line. Higher poles make the horse bend his joints more, creating more mobility through the body. Poles can be lifted on alternating ends, lifted just on the inside, just on the outside, or lifted on both ends.

WHY

- Poles with the *inner* edges raised: increases flexion of the inside hind leg, retraction of the inside shoulder, encourages bend, helps balance the front end, and increases scapula glide. This exercise is helpful for horses that fall in.

- Poles with the *outer* edges raised: mobilizes the scapula, engages the *latissimus dorsi* on the outside of the body, helps balance the front end, engages the *oblique stabilizing muscles*, and encourages lift/flexion/activity in the outside hind limb.

- Poles with alternating edges raised: increases proprioception and balance, engages the abdominals and loosens the back.

- Poles with both edges raised: the higher the pole, the more the horse must bend his joints and spring up while maintaining an even tempo.

- Raised ground poles help to de-weight the front end and transfer that weight to the hind, creating a lighter forehand, swinging back, and improved hind-end strength and pelvic stability.

- Horses learn to balance themselves and gain confidence over raised poles. This is an excellent exercise for one-sided stiffness and identifying weak pelvic muscles.

for Raised Ground Poles on a Bend

- ➤ Encourage a long-and-low headset, consistent tempo and slight inside bend.

- ➤ Maintain steady contact with the longe line.

- ➤ Start with fewer poles and add more to increase difficulty.

- ➤ You can play with different formations of your ground poles, but try to keep spacing in the center of the poles consistent (fig. 7.9).

- ➤ Keep this workout short and sweet so your horse doesn't become lazy over the poles. Switch between poles and flatwork often, and change direction multiple times.

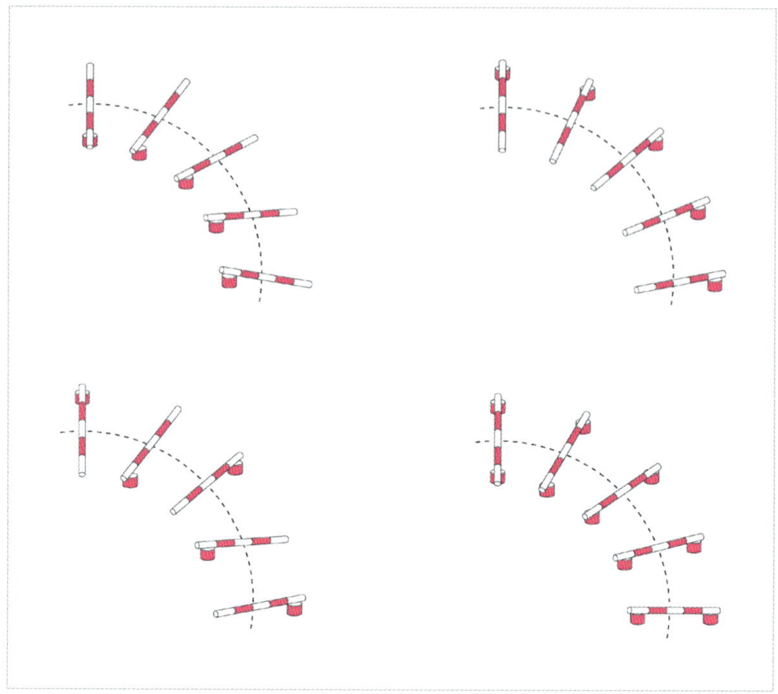

7.9 Here you can see ground poles raised on the inside, outside, alternate sides, and both sides.

HOW

1 Place 3–6 poles flat on the ground in a fan shape on a half-circle, roughly 3 feet apart for walking, 4–4 1/2 feet apart for trot work or 9–12 feet for canter work. You can also set up two circles of ground poles with different spacing on either side of your warm-up area in a Venn diagram shape in order to easily work between two gaits (see fig. 7.8, p. 118).

2 Start by warming the horse up at the walk and trot on a 20-meter circle, 5–10 minutes in each direction, near the poles but not over them.

3 After warming up, move the longe circle over and aim the horse toward the center of the ground poles, asking for an active and even walk, trot, or canter.

4 Once the horse has worked over the poles several times, raise them on the desired side (inside, outside, alternating ends, or on both ends) and repeat.

5 Make sure the horse doesn't drift toward the lower side of the poles and maintains a forward rhythm.

6 Start with the easier direction for your horse, but make sure to work both directions. Changing direction often is a good way to give your horse much needed breaks during the work.

7 Work over poles 4–6 times before reversing and repeat 3–5 times.

8 If you've set up two circles, switch between them before reversing. Allow the horse to rest for several circles away from the poles before repeating.

Common Issues and Precautions

- Keep poles around or below 6 inches high to discourage jumping over them.

- Aim for the middle of the poles. Don't be afraid to stop and adjust the spacing if needed in order to make the horse successful. Smaller strides target the *flexor* muscles while larger strides target the *extensor* muscles.

- If the horse is lacking strength or balance, try using 2–3 poles in a straight line instead of on a curve and allow them to navigate the poles while going straight, turning before and after the poles to complete the longe circle. You can also stop and hand-walk the horse over raised walk poles.

WHAT

Placing a cross-rail (or vertical) on your longe circle allows your horse to get comfortable jumping without the interference or weight of a rider.

WHY

- This is a lower impact exercise that helps your horse gain confidence and learn how to use his body correctly over fences.

- Improves the horse's ability to find his own distance to a jump.

- Strengthens the *thoracic sling* and supples the hindquarters.

HOW

1 Place a jump somewhere near your longeing area, with the inside of the jump low enough for the longe line to easily clear. This could be just a single pole raised on the outside or a jump set up with blocks (or even a mounting block) under the inside edge.

2 Warm up on a circle away from the jump for 5–10 minutes, in both directions.

3 Once warm, move the longe circle to include the cross-rail/jump and allow your horse to navigate his way over the jump as part of his circle (fig. 7.10).

4 Do not overdo this exercise and make it monotonous. Repeat 3–5 times before pulling the circle away from the jump.

5 Allow for ample rest before moving back to the jump and repeating.

6 Repeat each set of 3–5 jumps up to 5 times, reversing directions often.

---

tips **for Cross-Rail on the Longe**

- ➤ Aim for the center of the jump.

- ➤ You may need to raise the cross-rail if your horse doesn't actually jump it.

- ➤ Don't chase your horse over the jump—allow him to navigate and find his own distance and footwork.

- ➤ Maintain steady contact with the longe line and avoid pulling at the mouth when the horse jumps.

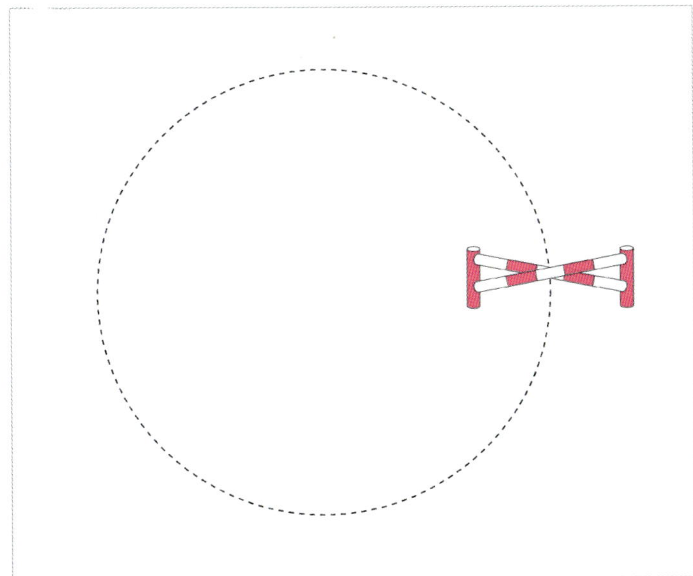

Common Issues and Precautions

- If the horse runs out at the jump, create a small chute or "wall" by placing a "v" pole on either side. This is a pair of ground poles, each with one end resting on top of the jump and the other end on the ground in a diagonal. This should help aim the horse to the middle of the jump.

- Do not attempt this exercise if there is a chance the longe line will get caught on the inside standard—you don't want your horse to feel punished for jumping.

chapter 8

Under Saddle

It is always a good idea to have a general plan for what you want to focus on or accomplish during each ride. When I work with human Pilates clients, I think about what I want to work on—for instance, "leg day" or balance training—and then I decide which exercises will best accomplish my goal after watching how the clients move on that specific day. If they are stiff, I will modify my program to include extra flexibility work. If they look strong and healthy, I may include an extra challenge.

Just as with humans, I go into my rides with a basic framework of what I'd like to accomplish, but I stay flexible and modify based on how my horse is feeling on the given day. Consider these exercises as tools in your toolbox you can pull out and use for your horse as needed, based on your goals and how he is feeling as you warm up.

8.1 Ridden work is where the fun begins! Start with a long warm up to let your horse's muscles loosen up before picking up a stronger contact and asking your horse to hold himself together. Concentrate on having a light and balanced seat to help support your horse as he works to move freely from back to front.

WHAT

These riding exercises are for both strength and mobility, and useful for all levels of rider. They are not meant to be done all in one day so pick and choose which ones will benefit your horse on a given day, and experiment with pairing various exercises to keep your horse fresh and progressing.

WHY

- No matter your specific riding discipline, these are exercises that any rider can incorporate into a horse's training program for full-body health benefits including core engagement, flexibility, and strength of the back and hindquarters.

- While there is no substitute for a good trainer, these exercises can be used by most riders on a regular basis and in between lessons.

- These exercises are meant to enhance the horse's natural way of going by creating strong but also long and supple muscles.

TOOLS

- A good trainer is an essential tool when beginning a new program under saddle.

- Make sure you have a properly fitting saddle and are working with the best bit for your horse—I like a full cheek or eggbutt double-jointed lozenge snaffle, but every horse is different. After two years in a 5 1/2 inch, 18mm eggbutt snaffle, I finally switched to a 5 1/4, 14mm eggbutt snaffle and my horse seems much more comfortable. Bit type and fit are important! Ask your dentist about the shape of your horse's mouth to determine size, and check with a trainer or fitter if you're unsure where to start with bit experimentation.

- A dressage whip can be helpful for some of these exercises, but is not necessary.

WHEN

It is better to ride more often for shorter amounts of time than to have a long, hard session once or twice a week. Ideally, you can ride 3–5 times a week with supplemental in-hand and longeing work. Try not to work on the same exercises several days in a row. Give your horse time to rest and recover by cross-training and working on different muscles or activities each day.

The Walking Warm-Up

WHAT

This is 10–20 minutes of walking at the start of your riding session with loose or light rein contact to help warm up your horse and prepare him for work.

WHY

- Walking mobilizes the spine, raises the body temperature, and increases circulation of fluids throughout the horse's body.

- This warm-up will help to release the core, stretch the spine in all ranges of motion (lateral, vertical, rotational), increase coordination and range of motion in the limbs, and relieve stiffness.

- It takes about 15 minutes to get synovial fluid moving, which is essential for the protection of cartilage in the joints. Blood must also begin to pump to the extremities, making them more elastic and taking stress off the tendons.

- The contraction and relaxation cycle of this warm up is also a low-effort way to recruit the small muscles of the topline.

HOW

1 Start by walking on a loose rein around the arena or field.

2 If you do not trust your horse to stay calm, hold the reins with light contact where the horse can reach into the bit but is not tense or held back.

3 If you trust your horse to walk on a long rein calmly (and you're in an arena), you can use this time to do mobilization exercises for yourself, stretching and circling your arms, shoulders, torso, and legs. It can be helpful to place your whip under your thigh and hook your reins over it to keep them from sliding down the neck.

tips for the Walking Warm-Up

- ➤ A 20-minute walking warm-up can reduce the chances of tendon and ligament injury.

- ➤ Lymph does not have a "pump," so muscles must contract and release to get the lymph flowing—essential for protecting the joints.

- ➤ Engage your core and sit properly in the saddle while walking—resist the temptation to relax into the saddle.

4 Halfway through your warm up you can pick up the reins for a slight amount of contact and start asking for transitions within the gait, lengthening and then bringing back the walk, and some gently bending. Do not ask for round, just ask for forward.

5 Add 10-meter circles, serpentines, and leg-yields to further warm up at the walk before beginning the rest of your work (fig. 8.2).

8.2 I keep a light contact and let Mark walk freely to start our ride. I try to sit lightly in the saddle so his back can relax, move, and warm up.

Common Issues and Precautions

- Try to plan enough time to warm up in all circumstances, especially before lessons when the work may be more difficult than during a usual schooling, but even when the planned work will be relatively easy.

- If your horse is nervous and won't settle, try keeping him busy with bending to the inside for a few steps and then to the outside a few steps, or add lateral movements early on.

- Walk-to-halt transitions can help awaken the horse to your aids if he is not listening or is distracted.

- You can also hand-walk your horse for several minutes to warm up before mounting.

Walk-to-Canter Warm-Up

WHAT

After warming up at the walk, some horses benefit from transitioning directly to canter. This is still considered the "warm-up," so don't ask for collection, tight circles, or other potentially difficult tasks the horse's body is not yet ready for.

WHY

- Cantering early in the session releases the horse's back and is less strenuous on the joints and feet than trotting.

- Creates flexibility in the lumbosacral joint, allowing the pelvis to rock and energy to flow more freely from the hind legs.

- Every upward transition is a contraction of the *intercostals/abdominals*, similar to a sit-up.

- This is a good warm-up option for horses that are prone to back pain.

HOW

1 If your horse is comfortable with walk-to-canter transitions, you can ask for the canter from an active walk. If not, pick up the trot for a few strides before asking for the canter.

2 Place a slight amount of weight onto the inside seat bone, your inside leg at the girth, and your outside leg slightly back, maintaining a balanced vertical body position to ask for canter. Do not fall back and pull with the reins as the horse reacts to canter.

3 Once in the canter, rise up to a half-seat to relieve pressure from the horse's back.

8.3 Try to stay light in the saddle without tipping too much weight forward during the canter warm-up.

4 Let the reins be slightly loose so the horse has freedom to lower his head and stretch through the neck and back (fig. 8.3).

Common Issues and Precautions

- If your horse has a tendency to get heavy on the forehand, skip Step 4 and maintain connection.

- For some horses, early canter work can take their focus away and amp them up. This might not be a good exercise for them at this time.

- Do not ask for the canter from a relaxed warm-up tempo. Pick up an active—but not rushing—walk or trot to prepare for the transition.

- Start with your horse's stronger lead, but make sure to canter in both directions.

The Stretch

WHAT

Spend some time during every riding session allowing your horse to stretch down and carry his head in a long-and-low position. This means allowing your horse's head to lower below the withers with the nose between chest and knees while maintaining balance through the rest of the body.

WHY

- When your horse's head lowers, the *nuchal ligament* and neck create upward force on the *spinous processes* in the withers, which then pull the rest of the spine up. This allows the lower back and sacrum to also lift and places the *longissumus dorsi* under gentle traction as the spine rounds and the pelvis tucks. This creates both a strong and supple horse, essential for a proper "frame."

- A high head and hollow back will create extension in the *lumbosacral* joint, blocking the stifle from strengthening. Working long-and-low will help release any restrictions created from overly activated muscle chains used when the horse works high and hollow, and allow for proper muscle activation and strengthening to take place.

- While an overly shortened neck can restrict hip movement, a long neck encourages hip extension and mobility.

HOW

1 Start by riding with connection, asking for work that engages the hind end and lifts the forehand like **Spiraling** (p. 111), **Leg-Yield** (p. 148), **Turn on the Haunches** (p. 145), and **Serpentines** (p. 132), for example. This will balance the horse so he doesn't fall heavily on the forehand when stretching.

2 Sit lightly in the saddle so your horse's back can rise and his hind legs can reach under.

3 Slowly allow your horse to "chew the reins down," releasing your fingers lightly without throwing the reins forward (fig. 8.4). Allow your hands to lower slightly.

4 Maintaining contact is essential: do not push the reins forward or throw the reins away to ask your horse to stretch.

8.4 Ideally, your horse's head lowers without his weight dropping onto the forehand. Mark loves to stretch down but usually that also means he is pulling with his front legs instead of pushing from the hind. We must wait until he has worked properly from the hind and through the back to find a more balanced stretch. It is a work in progress.

Common Issues and Precautions

- Try releasing to the stretch at the walk first, and then on a circle. It can also be helpful to ask for the stretch at the end of a session, when your horse is more likely to stay balanced and want to stretch his back.

- Keep yourself upright and resist the urge to tip forward which can throw your horse on the forehand.

- Do not let your horse fall onto the forehand in the stretch. If he gets heavy in front, try doing some lateral work, serpentines, and other bending movements to engage the back so you have an idea of what the balance should feel like before returning to the exercise.

Serpentine

for the Serpentine

➤ Maintain a forward and active rhythm and consistent contact.

➤ This is a good exercise for horses that hurry or lose rhythm in the turns.

WHAT

Riding a serpentine means making large loops or a series of half-circles around the arena forming an "S" shape. Ask for a change of bend after each loop without your horse's head rising or the speed increasing.

WHY}

- Creates dynamic flexibility through the rib cage.

- Strengthens the core muscles including the *supraspinatus, infraspinatus, pectorals, intercostals, mutifidus,* and *brachiocephalic* muscles.

HOW

1 Start with a medium walk.

2 Know the size of your arena so you can make equal loops of three to start, or four for a more challenging version (figs. 8.5 A & B).

3 Begin your serpentine in the middle of the short side of the arena and

ride a half-circle with the horse bent around your inside leg, supported by the outside rein.

4 The inside rein does not pull, but asks for a small amount of flexion.

5 Place your outside leg slightly behind the girth to control the hindquarters from swinging out.

6 Your horse should walk straight through the center of the arena, parallel to the short side, for roughly one horse's length. Half-halt to rebalance before changing the bend and repeating the next loop or half-circle.

7 Once perfected, try the serpentine pattern at the trot.

8 For additional challenge, you can try serpentines at the canter with a simple change of lead, utilizing the counter-canter, or with flying lead changes.

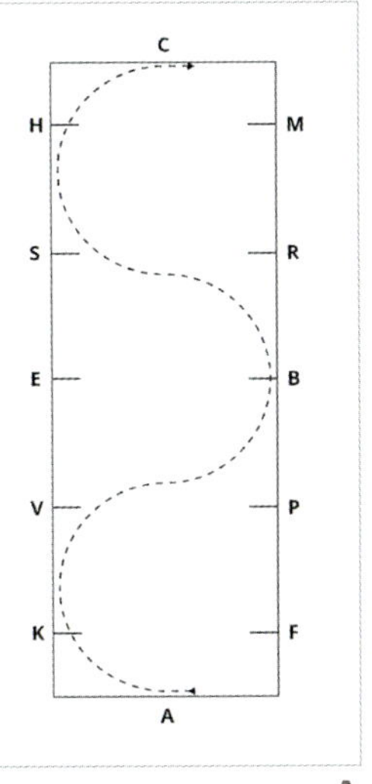

A

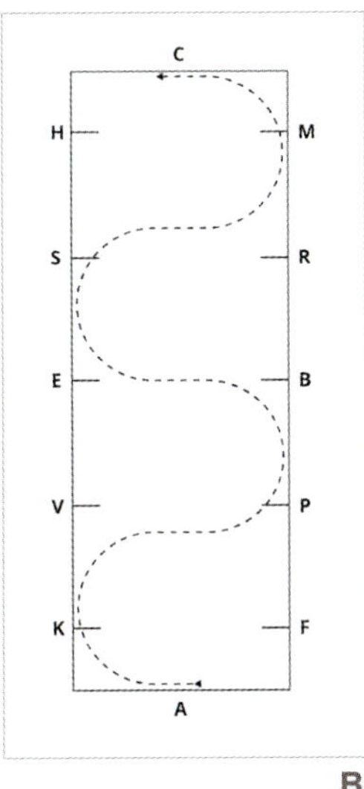

B

8.5 A & B The serpentine with three loops (A) and four loops (B).

Common Issues and Precautions

- If you're having trouble with the bend, try riding a figure eight first. Practice spiraling (see p. 134), or close off each loop by making a full circle before moving on.

- Do not ride deeply into the corners; ride half-circles.

- If your horse is falling out with his shoulder, try keeping your loops several feet off the track to keep him from using the rail for support.

- Your horse may resist more to one side at first because this exercise requires a lot of balance. It takes time to perfect, so be patient.

- Try to sit tall and don't lean through your corners. This can throw your horse off balance.

- Place two cones to travel through on the straight line of each serpentine to ensure you work straight before changing the bend.

WHAT

Spiraling under saddle requires your horse to move on a circle, gradually decreasing the size from 20 meters down to 15 or 10 meters before increasing back to 20 meters and repeating.

- Try to maintain a consistent rhythm and inside bend.

- Begin by asking for only 1–2 steps out at a time before moving forward again.

WHY

- Creates suppleness and balance, encouraging a lift of the horse's rib cage and conditioning of the core.

- Increases the engagement of the hind end, especially the inside hind leg.

- Increases reaction to rider aids, especially inside leg pressure and outside rein connection.

- Spiraling in is a good precursor to collection and spiraling out is a good precursor to leg-yielding.

HOW

1 At the walk or trot, start on a 20-meter circle with a forward-thinking rhythm and a slight shoulder-in.

2 After one or two circles, gradually decrease the size of your circle to 15 meters by increasing pressure with the outside rein and leg until you feel your horse moving in.

3 Maintain the inside leg to stop your horse from bending outside and use your outside leg to keep the haunches from drifting out.

4 Always be mindful of forward impulsion.

5 Decrease the circle down to 10 meters before gradually increasing the circle again by applying the inside leg with soft pulses in time with the

rhythm of the gait. Half-halt as the outside hind leg touches the ground in order to balance the outside hind leg.

6 Maintain outside-rein connection to keep the outside shoulder from bulging.

7 Ask for one to two circles before closing the circle in again, repeating the same cues.

8 Think of a slight shoulder-in both when spiraling in and out. When spiraling in, this will help maintain the engagement of the inside hind leg. When spiraling out this will help your horse stay connected to the outside rein (fig. 8.6).

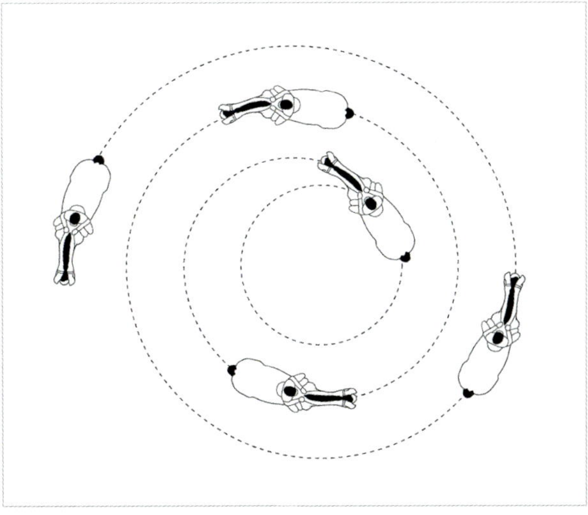

8.6 This illustration shows the path your horse should take when spiraling under saddle.

Common Issues and Precautions

- Make sure to spiral gradually and keep the connection to the outside of your horse.

- Encourage an active, forward horse with the inside leg to keep the haunches from falling in.

- Try putting cones at 20-, 15-, and 10-meter marks to keep track of your circle.

- If your horse is diving inside, drop to a slower gait and try again with slower progressions in and out on the circle.

for Long-and-Low Downward Transitions Between Gaits

➤ Think of the downward transition as gradual; do not surprise the horse with your request or aids.

➤ A downward transition is still a forward movement. Don't shut down impulsion with aggressive hands.

8.7 A & B When transitioning from canter **(A)** to trot **(B)**, you must make sure immediately to begin following the motion of the trot without getting left behind.

Long-and-Low Downward Transitions Between Gaits

WHAT

Move from a faster pace to a slower one such as walk to halt, trot to walk, or canter to trot, encouraging a low headset, ideally between the chest and knees.

WHY

• Engages the *spinal stabilizers* and *locomotion muscles* along the topline.

HOW

1 Begin by working with a low headset, allowing the horse to stretch forward and down.

2 Engage your core and increase the weight on both your seat bones as you discontinue following the motion.

3 Close your legs gently at the girth (or in the canter, inside leg at the girth while your outside leg closes just behind the girth) to encourage the hindquarters to come under the body and the front end to lighten.

4 Close your hands on the reins.

5 Immediately begin following the motion of the new gait (figs. 8.7 A & B).

- Try not to lean back or fall behind the motion.

- Prepare for every transition and think ahead through your steps before initiating the exercise.

- Don't let the horse get behind your leg.

- Practice half-halts to help your horse find balance.

- Try working on lateral exercises to engage the hindquarters in order to have stronger downward transitions.

- Asking for a slight inside bend can help release tension in your horse's neck.

Countdown Transitions

WHAT

Countdown transitions are progressively rapid transitions between gaits, starting with walk to trot. Begin with 10 strides of walk before asking for an upward transition for 10 strides of trot. Transition down for 9 strides of walk and then up for 9 strides of trot. Continue down to 8 strides of each gait, lowering the number of strides at each gait until you can complete one stride of both walk and trot. Advanced modifications can include transitions such as trot to halt, canter to walk, or lengthening and collecting within a single gait.

WHY

- Multiple transitions between (and within) gaits can help create a quicker neuromuscular response as well as increase coordination and proprioception.

for Countdown Transitions

➤ This exercise is best on a 20-meter circle. Transitions on a circle can help your horse balance back on the hindquarters more easily.

➤ Try to stay light in the saddle so that the horse can lift his back. Do not lean back or sit heavily to slow your horse as this can cause the back to invert.

➤ Go with the motion and don't brace against or block the movement.

- Helps disengage bracing muscles like the neck.

- Increases mobility and responsiveness in the hind legs and core.

- Downward transitions: transfers weight to the hind end, strengthening it.

- Upward transitions: strengthens the *core* and adds aerobic exercise.

HOW

1 Start at the walk, counting 10 steps.

2 Prepare for the trot around 7 or 8 steps, asking for the transition to trot by step 10.

3 At step 10 of the trot, transition back to walk.

4 Walk 9 steps and then transition back to trot.

8.8 A & B Mark and I are always working on a consistent connection, balance, and proper engagement through transitions from walk to trot and back again.

5 Trot 9 steps then transition to walk.

6 Walk 8 steps and then transition back to trot.

7 Trot 8 steps before transitioning again.

8 Continue transitions, dropping a stride each time until you have one stride of each gait. If a transition is sloppy, repeat that number until it is clean before moving on (figs. 8.8 A & B).

Common Issues and Precautions

- Always make sure to prepare for the transition and don't surprise your horse with an immediate or aggressive transition aid.

- Don't forget to use both your seat and leg in the downward transition to encourage flexion of the hock and stifle, which lowers the haunches and balances the horse's weight back. Keep your leg on as you transition downward and immediately follow the new gait with your seat so that you don't shut down the forward movement.

- Your seat and rein are important to encourage an uphill, smooth upward transition that has energy but not speed.

- If your horse starts to rush and throws his head up, come out of the exercise and regroup before asking for transitions again. It is more important to have relaxed transitions with the head steady than to complete the exercise steps perfectly.

WHAT

Maintain a steady tempo and rhythm but send more energy forward than upward to create longer, bigger strides. This means your horse should stay engaged and continue pushing from behind as he lengthens, covering more ground without getting faster. Try lengthening the stride along the long side of the arena and coming back to working on the short side.

tips for Lengthening the Gait

➤ You should feel increased suspension during lengthening work.

➤ Think about power and balance, not speed.

➤ Pick a spot in the distance to focus on and ask your horse to take you there.

WHY

- The most effective strength training aspect of lengthening is the "push" forward, so it is more beneficial to do several transitions than to hold an extended gait. This also increases circulation, which helps increase range of motion.

- Improves balance and suppleness.

HOW

1 Start with a steady working trot.

2 Stay balanced over the center of the saddle and try not to fall behind the vertical as you close your legs and ask for a push forward.

3 Soften your hands but maintain contact (do not throw your reins forward and let the horse fall on the forehand). Your horse should reach into the contact.

4 Send energy out in front of you while supporting the rhythm with your body so the trot becomes longer but the tempo does not quicken.

5 If your horse breaks to canter or falls on the forehand, half-halt to slow and rebalance before asking again. Do not pull on the reins and block the forward push (fig. 8.9).

8.9 Do not throw your reins forward or fall back with your body as you ask for lengthening. Engage your core and remember that if you do fall back, keep your hands independent and steady.

Common Issues and Precautions

- Some horses speed up instead of truly lengthening. Try placing two ground poles on the long side of the arena at an easy distance apart (6–8 strides). Pick up a working version of your chosen gait and count your strides between the poles. When you come to the poles again, ask for lengthening – there should be fewer strides the second time. If you count more strides, your horse may be speeding up instead of using bigger strides. Use more half-halts and check your connection. Could you be relaxing your hands forward as you add leg?

- Lengthening teaches your horse to use his body and neck to move into the hand. This means it's essential not to throw your reins forward when asking for an upward transition within the gait.

- This exercise can be a useful tool to calm a tense horse.

- It is common for the horse to break into canter when first learning to lengthen the trot. Do not punish him, simply transition back to trot, rebalance, and ask again.

tips for Counter-Canter

➤ Do not ride deeply into the corners before your horse is ready—it is challenging to maintain balance and rhythm and can be too difficult for the horse's outside hind leg to maintain the counter-canter through the turns.

➤ Keep a little more weight on your inside seat bone but do not lean.

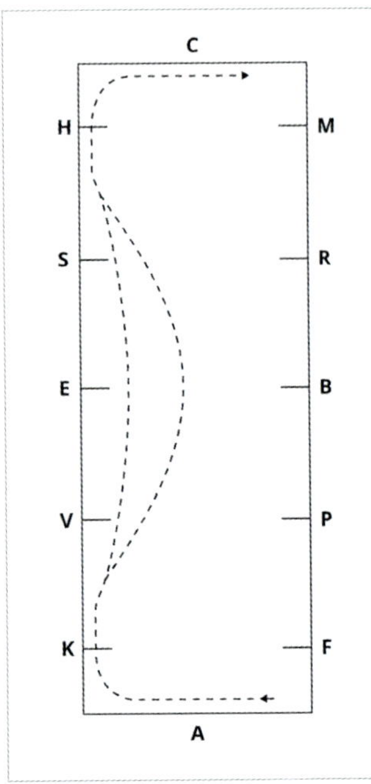

WHAT

Maintain a balanced canter on the outside lead. This means if you're tracking right, the horse is on the left lead for counter-canter.

WHY

- Increases balance, suppleness, and straightness.

- Strengthens the horse's *abdominals* and lower back as the pelvis tucks under.

- Hips are more weighted than in true canter, strengthening the hind end.

HOW
Exercise 1

1 Start by cantering in a long, straight line, staying steady and balanced while maintaining the canter aids—slightly more weight on the inside seat bone, outside leg behind the girth, inside leg keeps forward motion at the girth, and the outside rein stays steady and maintains straightness through the outside shoulder.

2 Gradually move off the rail to the quarterline, cantering a few strides before gradually moving back. Maintain a consistent rhythm while creating this shallow loop.

3 After your horse has comfortably executed this, try making the loop bigger (fig. 8.10).

8.10 Start with a shallow loop (the path closest to the rail) when beginning counter-canter work. After successfully completing this loop with a calm, consistent canter, make your loop larger, moving out to the centerline of your arena before moving back to the rail.

Exercise 2

1 After completing the first exercise successfully, ask for the correct canter lead down the long side of the arena.

2 At the corner, make a large half-circle—or cross the short diagonal—and come back toward the rail in the counter-canter.

3 Stay slightly off the rail and round off the corners of the short side as if doing a half 20-meter circle in order to assist your horse with balance through the turn.

4 After riding the short side, cross the diagonal to come back to the canter on the correct lead and then transition back to trot. This step is important when first teaching your horse to counter-canter so that he doesn't begin to anticipate breaking to trot from the counter-canter (fig. 8.11).

Common Issues and Precautions

- Riding somewhat forward (but not rushing) is helpful for a horse having trouble maintaining the counter-canter.

- A slight shoulder-in can assist with straightness, but avoid exaggerated flexion.

- If your horse switches leads or cross-canters, come back to trot, pick up the correct lead, and find balance before attempting again.

- If struggling to maintain rhythm or tempo, make your patterns larger.

- Do not attempt these exercises before finding a balanced and engaged correct lead or "true" canter.

- This exercise can be difficult to execute properly if you're not relaxed and accurate with your aids and able to maintain an independent seat.

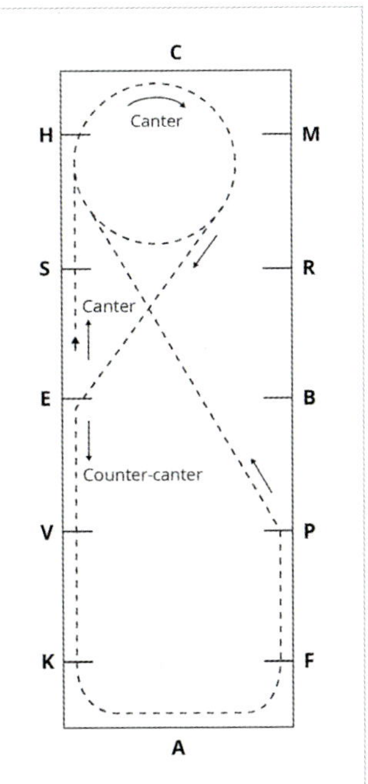

8.11 This is a helpful pattern to use when introducing your horse or yourself to counter-canter work. Pick up the canter at E, or any letter down the long side, and find a balanced and consistent canter before cantering a large half-circle, or crossing the short diagonal and traveling back to the rail at the counter-canter.

WHAT

This exercise requires the horse to cross his back legs and turn around a pivot point next to the inside foreleg (the side closest to the rail if you're moving the hind legs away from the rail), while the front legs step up and down in a walk rhythm. Essentially, you are changing direction by asking your horse to move away from your leg with his hind end, while staying relatively still with his front end.

WHY

- Mobilizes the rib cage.

- Engages the *deep vertebral* muscles and stretches the *gluteals*.

- Relaxes the *extensor chain* (topline).

- Increases suppleness, coordination, and response to lateral movement aids.

- A good preparation for leg-yielding.

HOW

1 Start in a square halt.

2 Bend your horse's poll (not the entire neck) slightly toward the rail, which is now considered the inside, and shift your weight onto the inside seat bone.

3 Place the inside leg (leg closest to the rail) just behind the girth and ask your horse to move his hind end away from the pressure.

4 Your horse should move his hindquarters away from the rail and around the forehand to face the other direction, crossing his back legs and stepping up and down almost in place with his front legs.

tips for Turn on the Forehand

➤ Do not pull on the inside rein and create a bend from the withers—this can throw your horse's balance too far over the outside shoulder and create drift.

➤ Make sure you have enough room to change direction if working on the rail.

8.12 The arrow at the rider's right leg indicates the importance of the "inside" leg aid to ask the horse's hind-quarters to move. The horse's neck is bent slightly to the inside, and the front end rotates in relatively the same spot as the hind end moves in an arc around it.

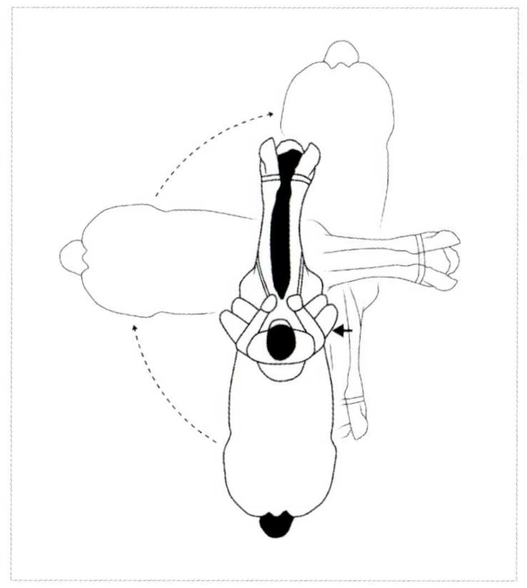

5 The outside rein supports the straightness of the neck, stops the shoulders from falling out and prevents forward motion.

6 Start by asking for only 2–3 steps instead of a full change of direction before walking forward as a reward (fig. 8.12).

Common Issues and Precautions

- If your horse backs up or throws his head up in confusion, try working on **Criss-Cross In-Hand** (p. 101) first.

Turn on the Haunches

WHAT

This exercise requires your horse to cross his front legs and turn in a small half (or full) circle around a pivot point close to the inside hind leg, at the walk. As the front legs cross, the outside hind leg makes a small arc (up to 3.3 feet long) around the inside hind leg, which steps in place. Essentially, you are changing direction by asking your horse to move with his front end while staying relatively still with his hind end.

WHY

- Increases suppleness, strength, and balance as well as responsiveness to the aids for lateral work.

- Frees the shoulder and increases range of motion in the *thoracic sling* to lift between the shoulder blades, pushing the front end up and allowing more space for the hind to engage.

- Engages the pelvis and hindquarters and strengthens the *abductor* and *adductor* muscles.

- Creates flexion in the supporting inside hind leg and extension in the outside hind leg.

- Engages the core.

HOW

1 Start with a medium walk with a slight bend toward the direction the front legs will move.

2 Begin to shorten the walk in preparation, but stay active.

8.13 This illustration shows how the horse's body should move in Turn on the Haunches. The neck is bent slightly in the direction of travel and the front end moves in an arc as the hind end rotates in relatively the same spot.

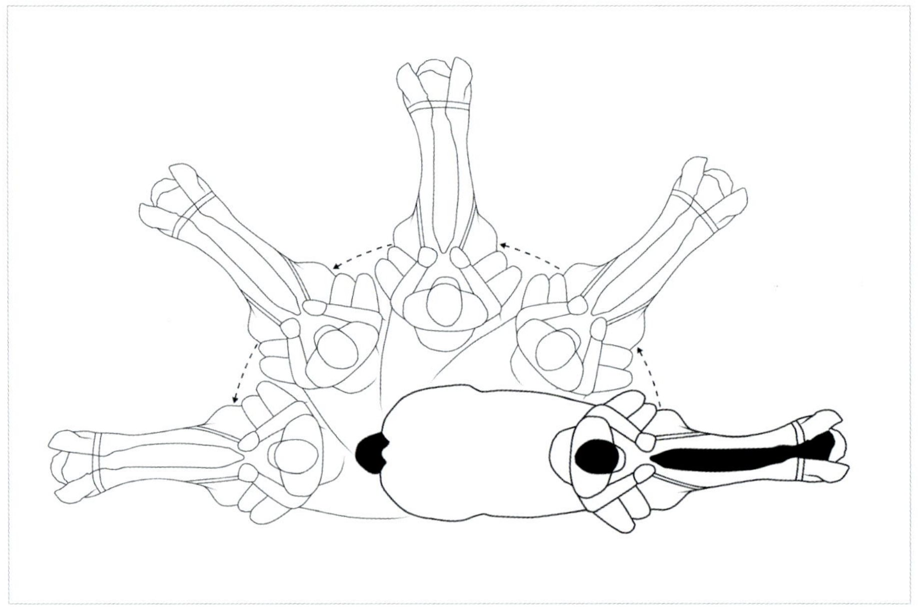

3 Place your inside leg close to the girth in a forward driving position, preventing your horse's inside hind leg from stepping in.

4 Place your outside leg behind the girth to prevent the haunches from falling out and to maintain activity.

5 Your inside rein leads into the turn while the outside rein prevents too much bend and allows the outside shoulder to turn.

6 The inside rein and outside leg should initiate the turn as the inner foreleg is reaching forward (fig. 8.13).

Common Issues and Precautions

- Make sure your horse is bent toward the direction of travel and not toward their stiffer side.

- Do not allow your horse to move backward—if stepping back, check that you are not using too much rein.

- If the horse pivots instead of lifting his legs, ask for a forward step with your inside calf.

- Do not lean to the outside to keep the haunches from falling out—this forces the horse to work harder to find balance.

Confused about the difference between turn on the haunches and a pirouette? The two movements are very similar; however, the back feet stay in almost the same place for a pirouette and they are allowed to move up to 3.3 feet to perform turn on the haunches.

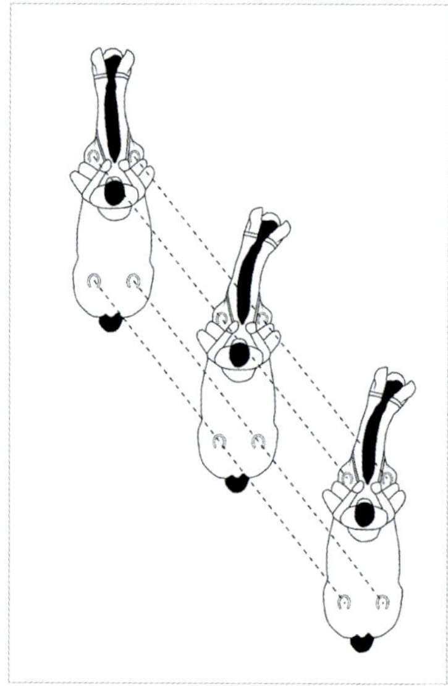

Leg-Yield

WHAT

The leg-yield requires your horse to move both forward and sideways, and is one of the first introductions to lateral movement. The horse should be mostly straight except for a small flexion at the poll away from the direction of travel. The forehand should move just slightly ahead of the hind end, and the inside legs should cross in front of the outside legs.

WHY

● Promotes suppleness and mobilization of the rib cage, loosens muscles throughout the entire body, and improves balance.

● Strengthens the *supraspinatus, infraspinatus, pectorals, intercostals,* and *obliques.*

● Engages the *deep vertebral* muscles and stretches the *middle gluteal* muscle while relaxing the *extensor chain* (topline).

HOW

1 Start with a straight, active walk down the quarter line or centerline.

2 Ask for a slight inside flexion just to where you can see your horse's inside eye and nostril.

3 Add a small amount of extra weight to your inside seat bone and ask for lateral movement toward the rail with your inside leg roughly 3 inches behind the girth, applying pressure as the horse's inside hind leg is about to leave the ground.

8.14 When performing a leg-yield, your horse's neck should be bent slightly away from the direction of travel as he moves both forward and sideways harmoniously.

4 Your outside leg is used to ask the horse to continue forward motion. Place it slightly behind the girth to prevent the haunches from swinging too far out.

5 Half-halts on the outside rein help maintain straightness and encourage balance on the outside hind leg (figs. 8.14).

Common Issues and Precautions

- Remember that your horse should have a slight bend opposite the direction of travel for this to be a true leg-yield.

- If the horse is behind your leg, try asking for a trot and then come back to an active walk before asking for lateral movement. Always think "forward" before thinking "over." This exercise can also be performed at the trot or canter.

- Keep your body perpendicular to the horse and don't collapse into your inside hip.

- If you have difficulty getting a response from your inside leg, try working on **Criss-Cross In-Hand** (p. 101). As your horse crosses his hind legs, tap your whip at his rib cage to encourage the lateral movement. Your horse should then associate the whip in this position as a cue for crossing the legs and you can then apply this same aid under saddle for similar results (fig. 8.15).

8.15 Mark crosses his hind legs in response to my inside leg applying pressure about 3 inches behind the girth.

WHAT

There are endless ways cavalletti and ground poles can be configured to benefit the horse. For our purposes, think of cavalletti as raised ground poles. As a general guide, poles should be placed roughly 3 feet apart for walking, 4–4 1/2 feet for trot work and 9–12 feet apart for canter work.

WHY

- Engages the core, thoracic sling, gluteals, and hindquarters, and increases spinal mobilization/swing.

- Encourages your horse to step higher and become more flexible in the joints as well as more sure-footed, increasing the quality of the gaits.

- Low impact strengthening exercise for the limbs.

- Helps maintain rhythm.

- Walking over cavalletti targets the *triceps, biceps, brachialis, extensor carpi radialis, gastrocnemious,* and *lateral digital extensor* muscles.

- Trotting over cavalletti targets the *trapezius, rhomboids, infraspinatus, lateral ulnar, lateral digital extensor, long digital extensor, common digital extensor, gluteals, bicep femoris,* and *semitendinosus muscles.*

- Cantering over cavalletti creates greater flexibility of the lumbosacral joint, which frees the horse to round the topline, which then stretches the tissue between the scapulae.

HOW

1. Carefully measure and set up your cavalletti exercise (see pp. 153–154 for examples). It's always a good idea to have 1–3 simple ground poles set up separately for warming up (figs. 8.10 and 8.11).

2. When possible, before mounting, walk over the exercise with your horse from the ground to make sure the spacing is comfortable.

3   Warm up on the flat and over the separate ground poles before going over raised cavalletti.

4   Find a consistent and quiet (but active) tempo.

5   Put your weight in the stirrups so you are not sitting heavily on the horse's back—be light to allow for maximum swing through the back and stay balanced in the center of the saddle.

6 Keep steady contact with the reins—do not throw your hands or weight forward when approaching the cavalletti.

7 Aim for the center of the cavalletti.

8 Use repetition to allow your horse to get comfortable over the poles and maximize benefit from the configuration, but don't overdo it. Repeat each exercise 4–5 times before taking a break (figs. 8.12 A & B–8.16).

Common Issues and Precautions

- Limit cavalletti work to 1–2 days per week.

- If having trouble with tension and consistency, add a small circle before the poles to encourage softness, bend, and stepping under with the hind end.

- If you cannot hold an even and quiet tempo with your horse's back relaxed and neck low, spend more time working over cavalletti at the walk, or start with only 1–2 cavalletti or ground poles.

- If your horse is consistently knocking the poles, alter the spacing to accommodate a more comfortable stride and focus on a relaxed and even pace—you may also need to work with body wraps (p. 176) to encourage better body awareness and proprioception.

- Placing cavalletti at the top height to encourage jumping can be beneficial, but that is more of a gymnastic exercise than what you are looking for here.

- Be careful when using old cavalletti with "X" ends. These can be dangerous for both horse and rider if the horse runs out. It's best to use cavalletti with square ends, or ground poles placed on risers.

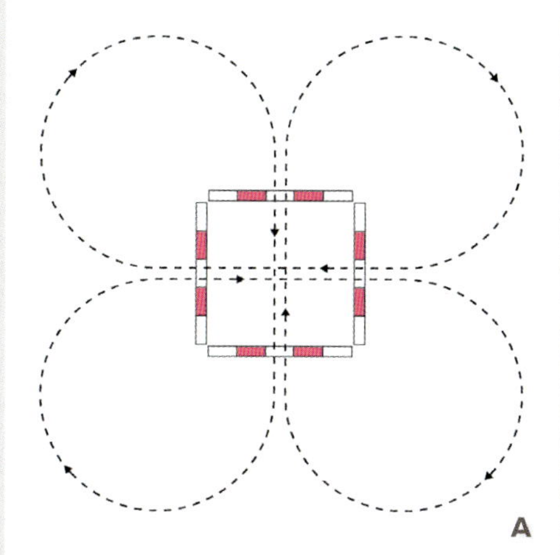

A

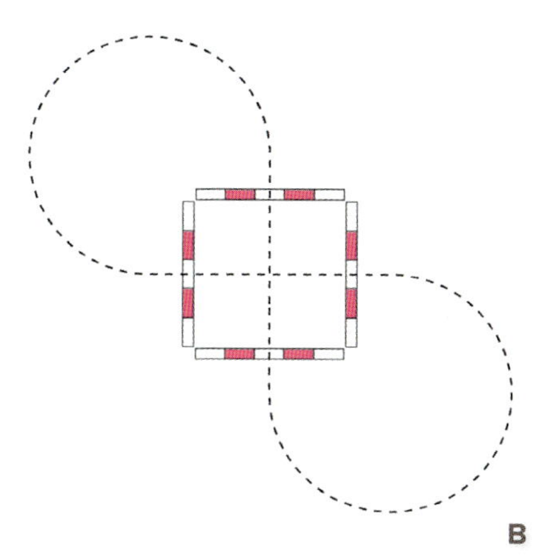

B

8.12 A & B This simple box setup is a great way to practice consistency in and out of elements. You can ride large circles over the cavalletti (or ground poles) following the path of the arrows, or you can make a figure eight over the poles to incorporate change of direction. You can also walk around the perimeter of the poles to practice square turns.

8.13 This is the spacing for working trot over cavalletti. This exercise challenges your horse's ability to maintain consistency when several poles are removed. Ride it in both directions.

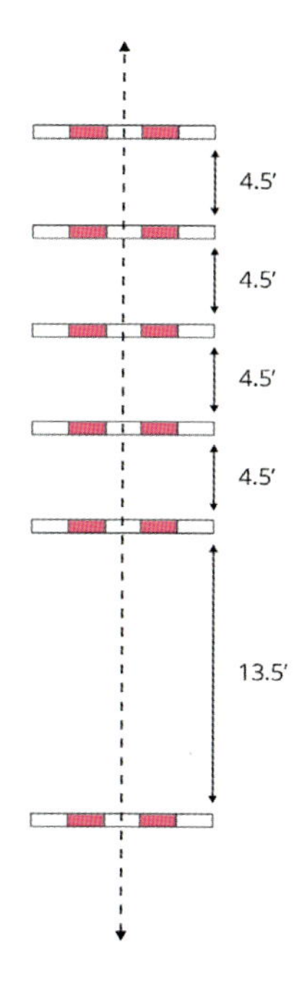

8.14 Angled cavalletti give you the opportunity to work on change of direction and bend over raised poles. This can be done at all gaits and is an especially challenging and rewarding exercise at the canter. Aim for the center of the poles as you ride

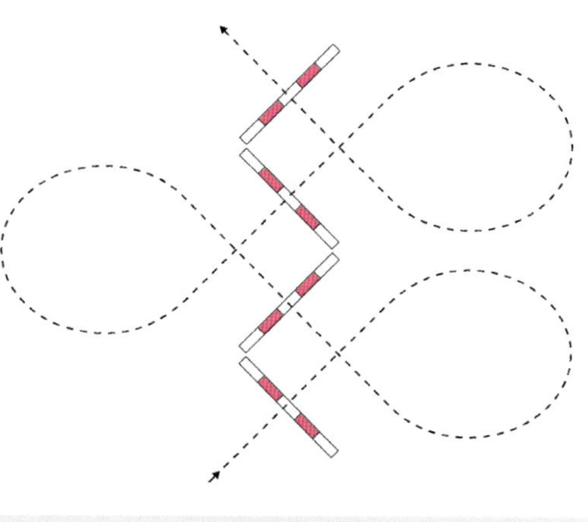

large figure eights over the poles in both directions. This configuration can also be simplified by trotting in a straight line through the angled poles from top to bottom, or making a small serpentine through the center of the poles as seen in Mini Serpentine Over Poles (p. 156).

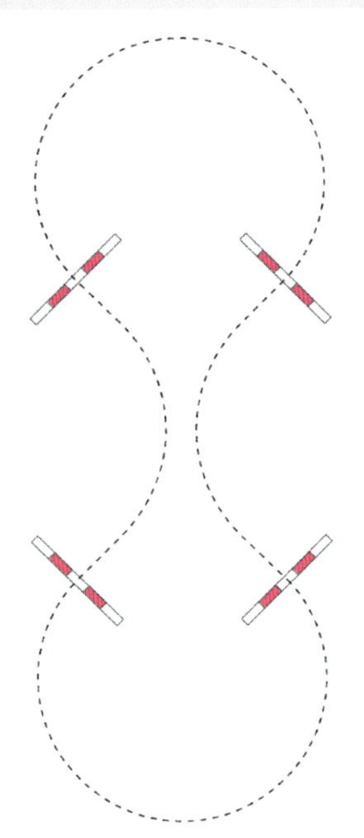

8.15 Cavalletti on an angle in a large box formation works on consistency through turns and change of bend. This can be done in loops as shown, or as a figure eight, at the walk, trot, or canter. I've even done this challenge bridleless to work on shoulder control.

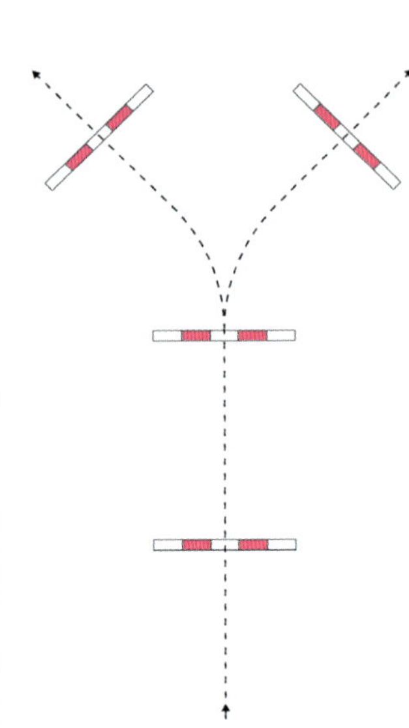

8.16 This configuration is especially helpful for horses that anticipate, and it is a good example of a single exercise design with multiple options once you're on the horse. This pattern can be ridden from the straight line to each bend, from the bend to the straight line, or directly through without the bending line. This is an excellent exercise for working on straightness, control, balance, and consistency at all three gaits. I find this to be a particularly challenging exercise at the canter when trying to work on maintaining my lead over poles.

Strength Circles

WHAT

Also considered cavalletti work, a strength circle is a 20-meter circle with 4 ground (or raised) poles placed at every quarter mark. This is a simple but effective exercise for both horse and rider.

WHY

- Teaches horse and rider to maintain a proper 20-meter circle.

- Encourages a consistent rhythm.

- You can work on lengthening over the widest part of the circle and collecting on the innermost part of the circle, which engages the hind end and both strengthens and supples the topline.

- Teaches the horse to not rush and to engage the hindquarters.

HOW

1 Measurement is crucial for this exercise—a 20-meter circle is 66 feet across. Use a measuring tape if available. If not, you can mark 33 feet (10 meters) on a longe line, place it in the middle of the circle and walk in a large arc around it holding the end of the line. You can also simply mark the middle of your circle and walk 33 feet out to where the center of the ground pole will go at each quarter mark (fig. 8.17).

2 Pick up a walk, trot, or canter and find a steady rhythm before entering the circle.

3 When ready, enter your circle and aim for the center of each pole.

4 Repeat 5–6 times and rest.

5 Change direction and repeat.

Common Issues and Precautions

- If your horse is rushing, ask for a downward transition before each pole.

- Try not to throw your body or hands over the poles—stay consistent.

➤ Try to get the same amount of strides between each pole.

➤ Keep a light seat so your horse can flex and use his back freely.

➤ This exercise can also be done on the longe line.

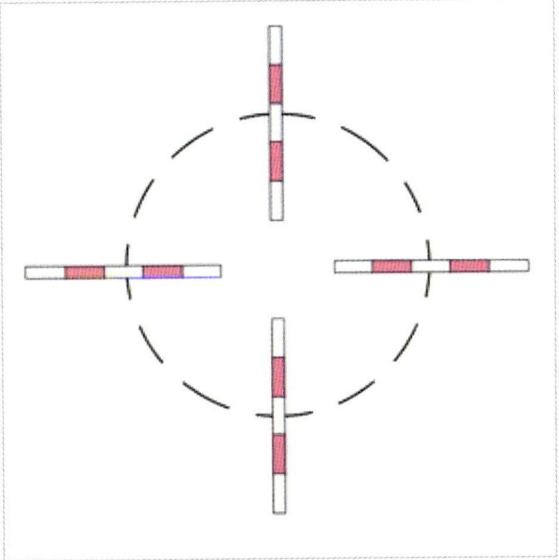

8.17 Place the center of each pole 33 feet from the middle of a circle to create a perfect 20 meter circle. Not only will this exercise help with consistency, but it will help you work on the ever-elusive shape of the 20-meter circle.

tips for Mini Serpentine Over Poles

➤ Raise the poles for increased difficulty.

WHAT

Line up several poles, either on the ground or lifted, in a zigzag pattern with the ends making a slight acute angle. Walk your horse in a tight serpentine, crossing over the poles at an angle before changing bend to the next pole. For a challenging modification, set the poles up end to end in one long line for a slightly tighter serpentine.

WHY

- Strengthens the small stabilizers of the pelvis and engages the thoracic sling.

- Encourages suppleness through the rib cage and a lift of the *abdominals*.

- Increases balance and proprioception.

HOW

1 Line up 4–6 poles in a loose zigzag pattern or straight line (figs. 8.18 A & B).

2 Start by walking the pattern with your horse from the ground so you can make adjustments if needed.

3 Keep the serpentine tight as you cross over the poles at a slight angle and change bend to face the next pole.

4 If crossing over one long line, stay close to the poles, and make very small loops back and forth.

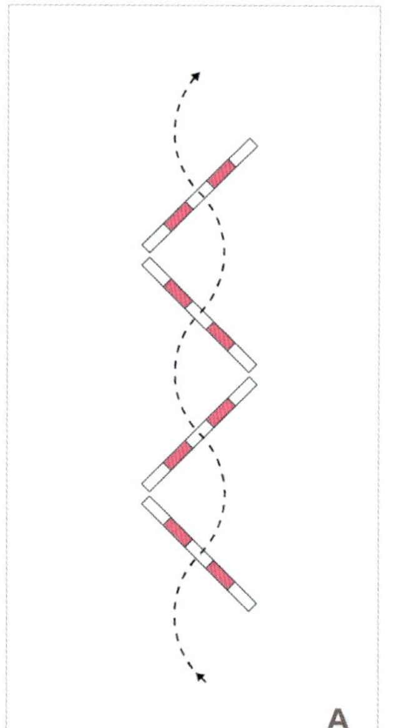

A

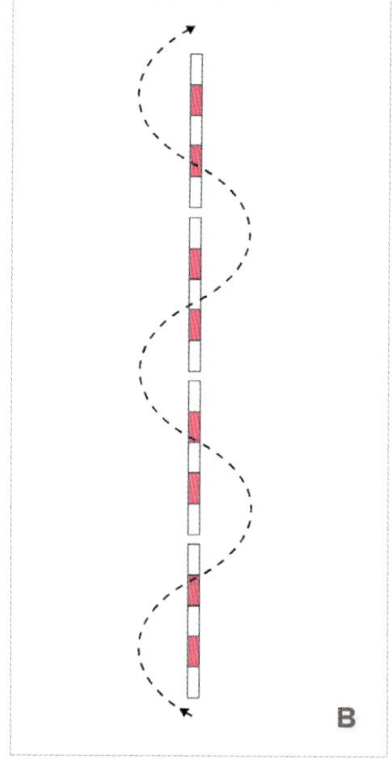

B

8.18 A & B Challenge your horse's suppleness by asking for a serpentine over angled poles (A). Ride across the poles at a slight angle before changing bend to the next pole. Placing the ground poles in a straight line is a more challenging modification for a tighter serpentine and greater angles over the poles (B).

- If you are feeling rushed or have trouble changing the bend in time, add more poles to make the line longer and make your loops larger.

- If your horse hits the poles consistently, come away from the pattern and find a more active and engaged rhythm before coming back to try again.

- Try using an Equiband® or body wrap (pp. 174 and 176) during this exercise.

Gymnastics

WHAT

Place two or more obstacles—for these purposes, jumps—a specific measured distance apart to work over. The possibilities for these gymnastics, much like cavalletti, are endless but a simple and effective place to start is 3 trot poles spaced 4 1/2 feet apart, to a cross-rail 9 feet away from the last pole, to a vertical or oxer 18–19 feet away.

WHY

- Since the distance of a gymnastic exercise is specific, repetitions allow the rider to focus on position as the horse figures out footwork. This helps both horse and rider jump better, improving agility, confidence, and overall technique.

- Strengthens the horse's ligaments, bones, and tendons.

- Excellent cross-training for all disciplines to help condition the body, flex the hindquarters, round the back, and reach through the neck.

- Verticals help create a tighter, more elevated jumping arc while oxers encourage the horse to stretch their arc over the jump.

- ➤ Think: calm, straight, balanced, attentive.

- ➤ Be precise with pole and jump placement specifically for your horse. Placing a rail roughly 9 feet (depending on your horse's stride) before a jump will help your horse place his feet correctly for takeoff. Jumps should be slightly closer together if trotting into the line, and farther apart if cantering into the first jump.

- ➤ The horse should slap the ground with his front feet, send his weight back onto the haunches, and flex the stifles, hocks, and sacroiliac joint to push off while the shoulder swings forward and the legs come up.

- ➤ The most efficient jumping form for the horse should include reaching the top of his arc as he passes over the middle of the jump, so takeoff and landing should ideally be the same distance from the jump on either side.

- ➤ Tighter distances will require the horse to bring his front end up more quickly while a longer distance encourages a more elongated body.

- ➤ Adding jumps will require more athleticism, balance, and coordination from your horse. This is a good way to challenge the hindquarters and help lighten the front end.

- Bounce jumps and cavalletti can be a useful addition to slow a rushing horse.

HOW

1 Place jumps with a measuring tape for precision. Start with 3 trot poles 4 1/2 feet apart to a trot pole 9 feet away (fig. 8.19).

2 Warm up on the flat, asking for transitions, spirals, and serpentines to supple the horse and get him on your aids.

3 Trot over the poles several times in each direction to establish a relaxed and clear rhythm.

4 Raise the last pole to a small cross-rail.

5 Add a vertical or oxer 18–19 feet away from the cross-rail at an easy height for your horse (figs. 8.20 A & B).

6 Approach the grid at a calm, regular and balanced pace.

7 Stay out of the way, sit tall, and allow your horse to navigate himself over the obstacles. It is your job to stay balanced and with your horse, and it's your horse's job to jump. Your head should remain at the same level down the line and you should look sequentially at each jump. Your seat should come out of the saddle similar to the rise of the posting trot. Do not fold over your horse's neck excessively or use the reins for balance. Grab mane if having trouble staying with your horse.

8 Raise the jumps slowly. You and your horse will benefit from this exercise even with low jumps, but

POLE PLACEMENT	PLACING POLE	BOUNCE	1 STRIDE	2ND 1 STRIDE	2 STRIDES
Trot Poles		4.5'			
Canter Poles		7'-10'	14'-20'		
Trot Approach	9'	9'-12'	~18'	19.5'-22'	28'-30'
Canter Approach	9'-10'	10'-12'	~21'	24'-26'	33'-35'

8.19 Use this distance chart as a general guide for your gymnastic. This is meant to be used for horses 15.3-hands or larger. The average horse stride is 12 feet. An extra stride is added when jumping to account for takeoff and landing. Many jump rails are also 12 feet, which can be helpful when measuring distances without a measuring tape. Schooling strides are most often smaller than competition strides, and you should adjust accordingly; however, it is better to err on the side of slightly too long than too short of a distance.

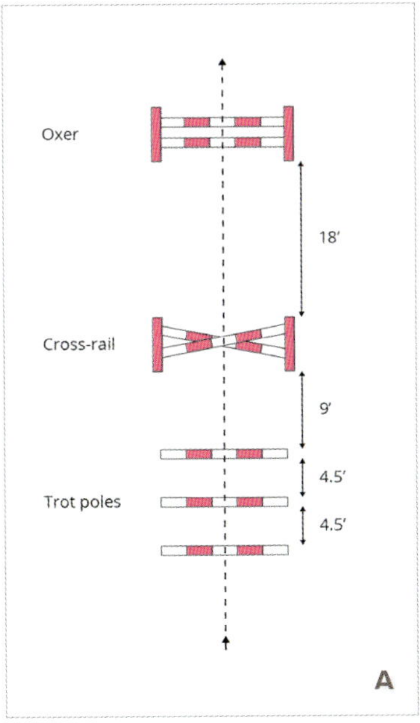

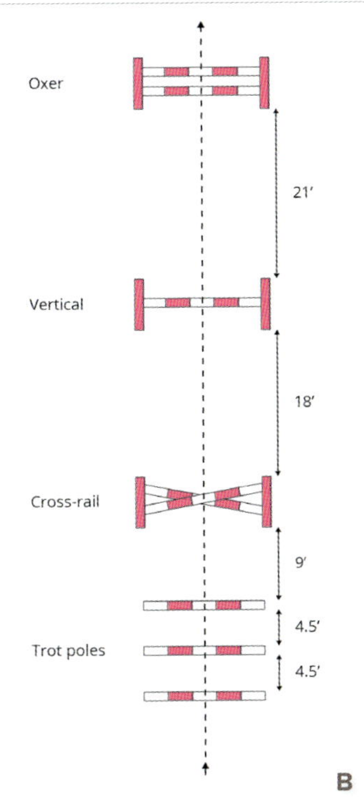

8.20 A & B This is one of the most common exercises to introduce a horse to gymnastics: Trot over three ground poles to a cross-rail, then on to a vertical or oxer (A). For increased difficulty, add more elements to your line (B). Note that when a horse trots into a gymnastic, you need to set the jumps for a shorter stride. As the horse moves through the line at the canter, his stride gets longer, which means later jumps should be set slightly farther apart.

a simple gymnastics line can also be a good place to practice jumping slightly higher than your current schooling level.

9 It is sufficient to begin with 4–6 repetitions.

Common Issues and Precautions

- Do not make a gymnastic higher and more complex at the same time. If you add an element, do not also increase the height simultaneously.

- Keeping the jumps low will still be beneficial for the horse and create less wear and tear on the joints and tissues.

HIIT

WHAT

HIIT stands for "high intensity interval training." These are training repetitions of high speed and high intensity work followed by active rest.

WHY

- HIIT will increase lung capacity, which allows for more oxygen to be delivered to the blood and increases endurance and efficiency.

- The fitter the horse, the faster the recovery.

HOW

1 Start on flat ground so that connective tissues aren't strained.

2 Warm up with 10 minutes of walk.

3 Canter 2 minutes.

4 Trot (or walk) 2 minutes.

5 Repeat 4 times.

8.21 When doing conditioning sets or HIIT workouts, it's best to work in a half-seat position to minimize the weight on your horse's back. Remember, proper work is efficient work so ride your horse back to front and don't let him drag you around the arena heavy on the forehand.

HEART RATE GUIDE	beats per minute (bpm)
Avg resting heart rate	35-50
Walk/trot work	~120
Long, slow work	140-160
Aerobic zone	160-180
Anaerobic threshold/gallop	200
Extreme short bursts	220

8.22 A basic guide to heart rate for HIIT workouts.

6 As the horse becomes more fit (after 3–4 weeks of consistent interval training) you can start to canter 6 minutes and walk 4 minutes for each interval. Advanced horses can modify to canter 8 minutes, walk 4 minutes. The work/rest ratio is dependent on your horse's cardiovascular fitness (fig. 8.21).

7 Finish this exercise with 10–15 minutes of walking.

Common Issues and Precautions

- Any work over 200 beats per minute (bpm), the anaerobic threshold, creates lactic acid and fatigue rapidly.

- This is not a good exercise for a completely unconditioned horse. If your horse has not been worked recently, start with 20–30 minutes of walking. Gradually increase to 20–25 minutes of walk/trot and then add HIIT as the horse becomes more fit.

- It can take an average of 3 months to reach peak cardiovascular fitness. The initial phase should be 2–3 weeks of slow buildup.

tips for HITT

- ➤ Use this exercise on conditioning days.

- ➤ Use a heart-rate monitor to make sure you are training the horse in the right threshold for his current level of fitness (see p. 38). A heart-rate monitor will also let you know if your horse is over-stressed by work or in pain for any reason (fig. 8.22).

- ➤ Adding HIIT sets on hills can increase both cardiac and strength gains.

- ➤ Your horse should always come back to regular breath before finishing the ride. The fitter the horse, the faster the heart rate and breath will go back to normal.

WHAT

This exercise requires the horse to step backward in a straight line, moving his feet in diagonal pairs.

tips for Rein-Back

➤ Maintain straightness and avoid a high headset by staying steady and not pulling with the hands.

WHY

- Rein-back asks the three major hind joints—the sacrum, stifle, and hock—to flex and bear additional weight, strengthening the back end while allowing the thoracic sling to mobilize and lift.

- The core activates and the flexor chain stretches and lengthens.

- Increases coordination of the body front to back and side to side.

- Working at slower gaits like the walk increases engagement of smaller muscles.

- Helps develop work through the back that is essential in collection.

- An especially helpful exercise when there is weakness in the stifles, tightness in the hamstrings, or the spinous processes (top of the spinal vertebrae) are too close or "kissing."

HOW

1 Make sure your horse has learned how to back up in hand as a preparation.

2 Stop in a square halt.

3 Sit lightly in the saddle to allow the back to lift.

4 Add a slight amount of pressure with both legs behind the girth.

5 When the horse begins to step, squeeze the reins firmly to ask for backward movement.

6 Ask for 3–5 steps at a time, although even one step should be rewarded when first learning this movement (fig. 8.23).

8.23 Keep a light seat as you ask the horse to step back. He should lift his feet, not shuffle, and move his legs in diagonal pairs backward.

Common Issues and Precautions

- Do not use the rein-back as a punishment.

- Don't force this exercise with a tense horse holding his head high or tucking his head too tightly to the neck. If you fight a high-headed, hollow, or tense horse in this exercise, he may feel stuck and rear up. It is best to dismount and solidify **The Back-Up** (p. 96) before attempting again.

- If your horse is hollow, check that the pressure of your hands is not too strong. Use your seat and legs to ask for the backward motion and use the reins only to keep the horse from moving forward.

- **Turn on the Haunches** (p. 146) can help unload the front end, and is, therefore, a good exercise to use before attempting to back up.

- Practice square halts before asking for backward steps.

tips for Uphill Work

- ➤ Trotting and cantering uphill is beneficial for full body conditioning and can be done after walking the hill several times.

- ➤ Sit lightly in the saddle to allow your horse to push from the haunches, but only lean forward if you have a tendency to be left behind or if the hill is particularly steep.

- ➤ Uphill work can also be done on the longe line or in hand.

- ➤ Modify for advanced horses by adding transitions within or between gaits—including transitions to halt—and by adding circles on the slope.

- ➤ Walking sideways on a hill is also a great way to engage the pelvic stabilizers, flex the horse's hind end, and strengthen the side of the horse that is uphill—great for one-sided dominance and stiffness in the hind.

WHAT

Riding up an incline.

WHY

- This is a concentric contraction of the hips, hamstrings, and glutes, which strengthens the hind end as well as the back, abdominals, and limbs.

- Engages the *longissimus dorsi, tensor fascia latae, semitendinosus, long digital extensor, gastrocnemius, deep digital flexor*, and *lateral digital extensor tendon*.

- The scapula rotates back in this exercise, which encourages larger range of motion.

- This is a good strength test. If your horse cannot maintain a slow and consistent tempo uphill, he needs more overall strengthening work.

HOW

1 Start by finding a gently sloped hill.

2 Begin at the walk and ask your horse to maintain a consistent speed as you move up the hill. Remain balanced in the saddle (fig. 8.24).

3 The slower you go, the more work the hind end will have to do.

8.24 Try to stay balanced in the saddle instead of tipping forward to encourage more work from behind.

Common Issues and Precautions

- If your horse must increase his speed or rushes to get up the hill, try to maintain a consistent trot tempo and work toward a walk as the horse gets stronger. You can also try to find a hill that is slightly less steep.

- The horse should push from behind, not pull from the front.

- Do not do hill work multiple days in a row.

- Avoid hill work if your horse has a stifle injury.

tips **for Downhill Work**

➤ Trotting downhill is good for full-body conditioning and can be done after walking the hill several times. When trotting, you may need to lean back slightly to stay in balance with the horse but be careful not to sit too deeply and drive the horse forward. Make sure the ground is not slick and your horse is shod appropriately for the condition of the footing before trotting hills.

➤ Sit lightly in the saddle.

➤ Modify for advanced horses by adding transitions within or between gaits—including transitions to halt—and by adding circles on the slope.

WHAT

Riding down a small hill or decline.

WHY

● Walking downhill transfers your horse's body weight forward onto the forelimbs as they perform an eccentric muscle contraction similar to collection. This creates strength in the small muscles of the limbs and their connective tissue, and is a good preparation for jumping.

● This exercise engages the core (abdominals) as the horse resists downward momentum.

● Strengthens the *biceps, brachiocephalicus, deltoid, supraspinatus, pectorals, brachialis, extensor carpi radialis, lateral ulnar, lateral digital extensor,* and *latissimus dorsi* muscles.

HOW

1 Start at the top of a gently sloped hill.

2 Begin at the walk and ask your horse to maintain a consistent speed as you move down the hill. Remain balanced in the saddle (fig. 8.25).

3 Slow and straight is key.

8.25 Much like traditional Pilates, the slower you go, the more work you will gain in the downhill exercise.

Common Issues and Precautions

- Any change in your balance means your horse must work harder to find his own balance. Be aware of your position at all times.

- Your horse may break stride at first and fatigue quickly. Allow him to work at his own pace until he is stronger.

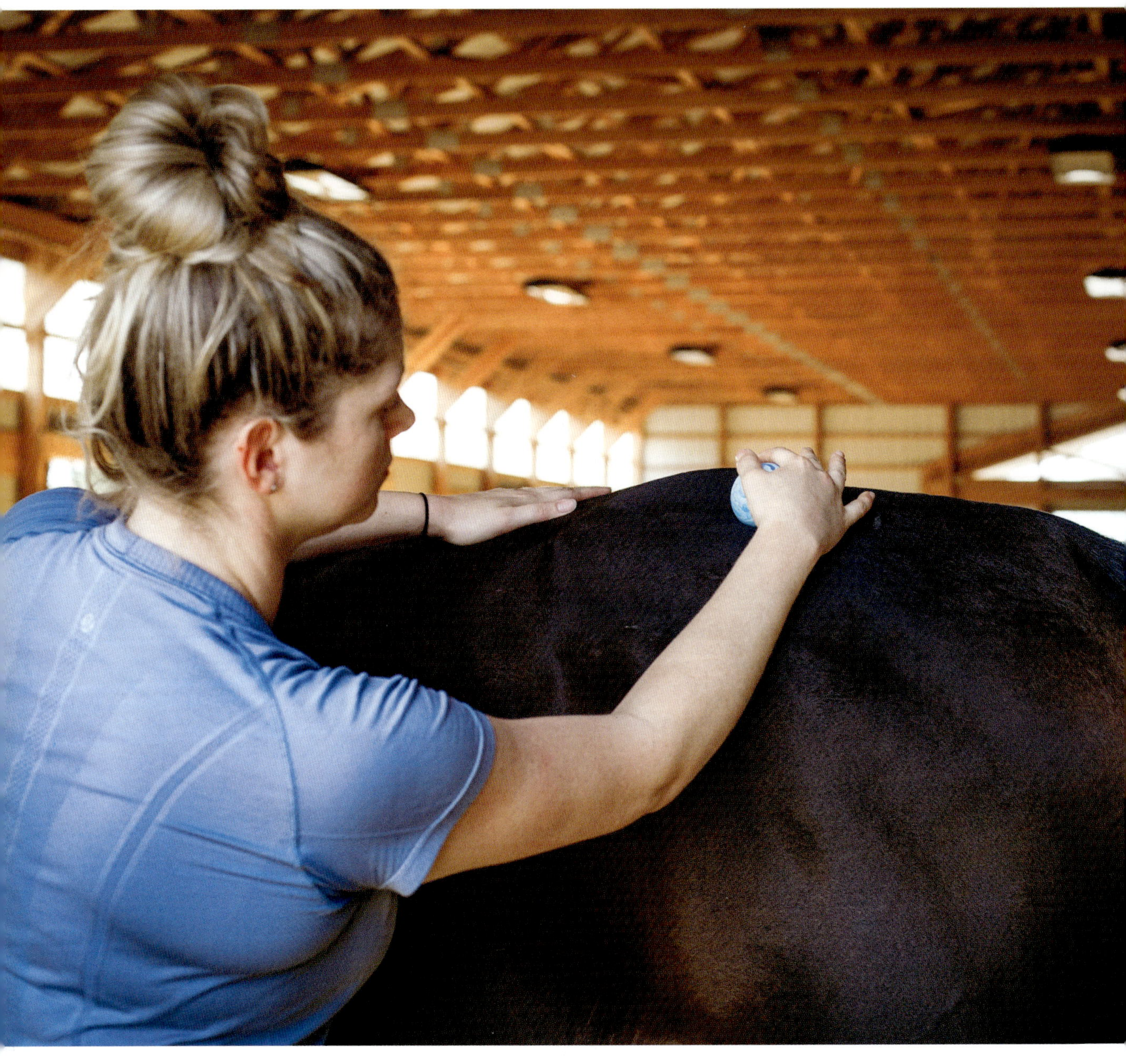

chapter 9

Alternative Bodywork

Alternative therapies can help increase the effectiveness of a core conditioning program by releasing tight and sore muscles and preparing the mind and body for work. The tools and techniques described in this chapter are amateur-friendly ways you can assist your horse in feeling his best. Whenever I have struggled with muscle strain or back pain in the past, I have used self-massage techniques, ice, and even a support brace to ease the pain. All of these ideas can be utilized for the horse as well.

9.1 Using tools such as a lacrosse ball, seen here in Lacrosse Ball Release (p. 172), can help release muscle tension or soreness, increasing mobility and enabling the muscle to be more easily recruited and strengthened during work.

WHAT

These techniques can relax both the mind and body, prepare the horse for work, help prevent injury, and assist in recovery after hard sessions.

WHY

- Muscles need rest and recovery as they build in order to stay long and supple. Horses are athletes and bodywork is an important part of all elite athletes' wellness programs.

- Many of these techniques have shown to be useful as both a preventive tool and as a complementary treatment to traditional medicine when rehabbing injuries by helping to reduce swelling and relax the muscles.

tips for Stability Pads

- Your horse may begin to rock back and forth, showing signs of relaxation and tension release. Allow him to do so for as long as he likes.

- Try adding incentive stretches (p. 55) or a weight-shifting exercise (pp. 84–87) while your horse is on the pad(s).

- Stability pads can be found online and they do not have to be made specifically for horses to work well. Bigger square pads are easier to use, but oval ones work as well.

- Try standing on the pad yourself to see how it changes your stability.

WHAT

Using a stability pad, such as those offered by Wendy Murdoch (SURE FOOT® Equine Stability Pads), under one or multiple feet can calm the nervous system and challenge your horse's balance and stability safely.

WHY

- Increases proprioception, motor control, and core stability.

- Allows the horse to find and release tension on his own.

- Activates the small stabilizing muscles surrounding the limb standing on the pad.

HOW

1 Allow your horse to see and sniff the pads before placing them under his feet.

2 Place a pad under one foot and allow the horse to get used to it. If he yanks his foot up, patiently reposition the pad and place the foot on it again. Don't force the horse to stay on the pad—stay patient and continue to replace the foot as needed.

3 Start with a front foot and work around to all four.

4 Once your horse is comfortable with one pad, try a second pad under another foot. Work slowly up to having all four feet on pads at the same time, if tolerated (fig. 9.2).

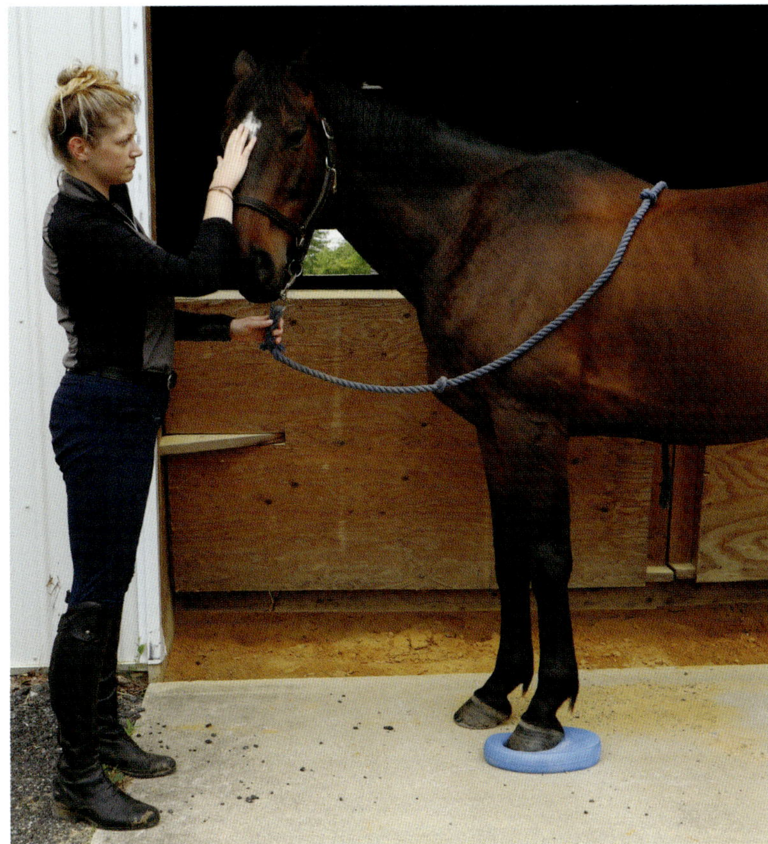

Common Issues and Precautions

- Do not try this on cross-ties. Allow your horse the freedom to move and get used to the new sensation of instability. This exercise is best done in a stall or arena.

- If your horse does not tolerate the pad, be patient. Continue to ask him to stand on the pad, but do not force it. If the horse will stand for just a few seconds, try to end by asking him to remove the foot instead of allowing him to pull away on his own, and give a reward. Try different feet to see if one is more comfortable than another.

WHAT

Roll a hard ball, like a lacrosse ball or tennis ball, in a slow, circular motion down and up the gluteal muscle from sacrum to hip to release tension. You can also use a Gua Sha stone (a tool used in Traditional Chinese Medicine) with good results.

WHY

- Releases knots and presses into trigger points/areas of tension that can get stuck or spasm.

- Mobilizes the fascia.

- Stimulates blood flow.

9.3 A–C Keep your hand open as you circle the ball around your palm along the horse's gluteal muscle (A & B). A Gua Sha stone is also an option for deep massage that is sometimes easier to use than a ball, but it is delicate and can shatter if dropped (C).

- *Gluteals* are often a compensatory muscle, meaning they engage as a stabilizer when the proper postural muscles/abdominals aren't activated. In order to release the cycle of dysfunctional movement, tightness needs to be released. This would be a good way to begin that process of release.

HOW

1 Place a ball on your horse's hind end, around the sacrum.

2 Use a flat hand on the ball to press into the horse's muscle, making small circular motions in an arc down toward the hip. Usually, you can see some muscling that will guide you along the top of the rump and down.

3 Roll the ball back up to the starting position and repeat.

4 Roll down and up slowly 3–5 times with moderate pressure, 2–3 times a week. Try to do equal repetitions on each side (figs. 9.3 A–C).

Common Issues and Precautions

- This is good for all levels of rehab except acute injury in the pelvis or hindquarters.

- If you don't have a ball, you can use the heel of your hand. I've also found that a gua sha or skin scraper, used only in the direction of the hair, works well to get deeply into the muscles and release tension.

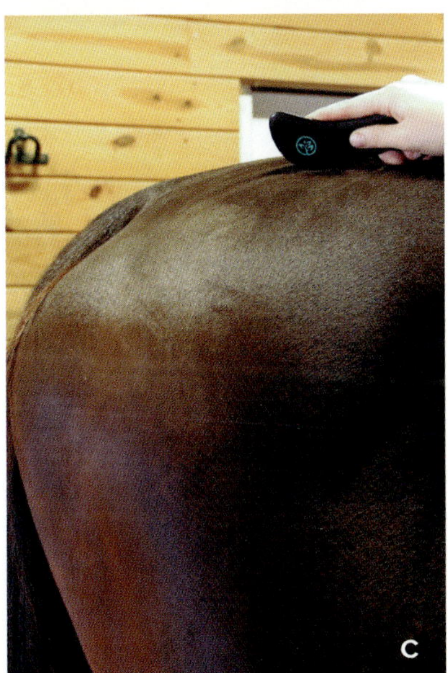

WHAT

The Equiband® is a saddle pad with two detachable resistance bands, one for behind the hindquarters and one for under the belly. It can be used in hand, under saddle, or on the longe line, and you can use one or both bands at a time. Ace bandages or polo wraps can also be used if an Equiband® is not available; however, you must be careful using other stretchy resistance bands that might not be as strong and could potentially snap.

WHY

- Bands stimulate receptors in the skin and hair, which help bring the horse's attention to the body parts being touched.

9.4 Once you have measured the bands for your horse, all you have to do is clip them into the saddle pad and go.

- The belly band activates the trunk muscles, encouraging a lift of the abdominals, which then gives the spine more ability to stretch and swing.

- The hind leg strap is meant to make the horse more aware of his hind-leg movement and help with coordination and proprioception.

- This is especially good for asymmetrical leg movement and strengthening underdeveloped muscles like the *biceps femoris*.

HOW

1 Start by desensitizing your horse to either the Equiband® or bandage, brushing the band around the belly and the hind end.

2 Have someone hold your horse when first introducing the bands, it may be a new sensation for him.

3 Start with just one band. Slowly fasten the band or bandage wrap (tied to the girth on each side and wrapped around the hind legs) halfway down and around the buttocks, between the top of the hip and the hock. Make sure the band is not hanging loose.

4 Hand-walk your horse to allow him to get comfortable with the tension before longeing or riding. Use the band from the beginning of your workout so the correct muscles can be engaged from the start (fig. 9.4).

5 Take off the hind band to repeat desensitization with the belly band.

6 Once both bands have been introduced separately, they can be used together.

7 Focus on transitions within the gait and between gaits for optimal use.

8 Expect your horse to fatigue early and make sure to rest often.

> Ride with bands every other day at first, reducing use over time.

9 Cut your work time in half, or take off the bands after working for 15–20 minutes when first working with them—the horse's muscles may be working harder than normal and will need time to recover.

Common Issues and Precautions

- If gait abnormalities get worse, stop using the bands.

- Do not put the bands on or take them off while in the saddle.

- Make sure the bands aren't hanging loose or too tight—bands should never be shorter than half the length between attachments to the saddle pad or girth on each side.

- Do not add bands after warming up—proper activation is needed at the beginning of the session.

Tellington TTouch® Body Wrap

WHAT

Use two large, slightly elastic bandages (such as Ace bandages or polo wraps) tied in a figure eight—one loop around the neck and one behind the rump—to create slings around the body that encourage a stronger mind-body connection.

WHY

- Enhances body awareness and proprioception through continuous sensory feedback.

- Increases balance, coordination, and confidence.

HOW

1 Allow your horse to sniff and get used to the feeling of the bandages on his skin.

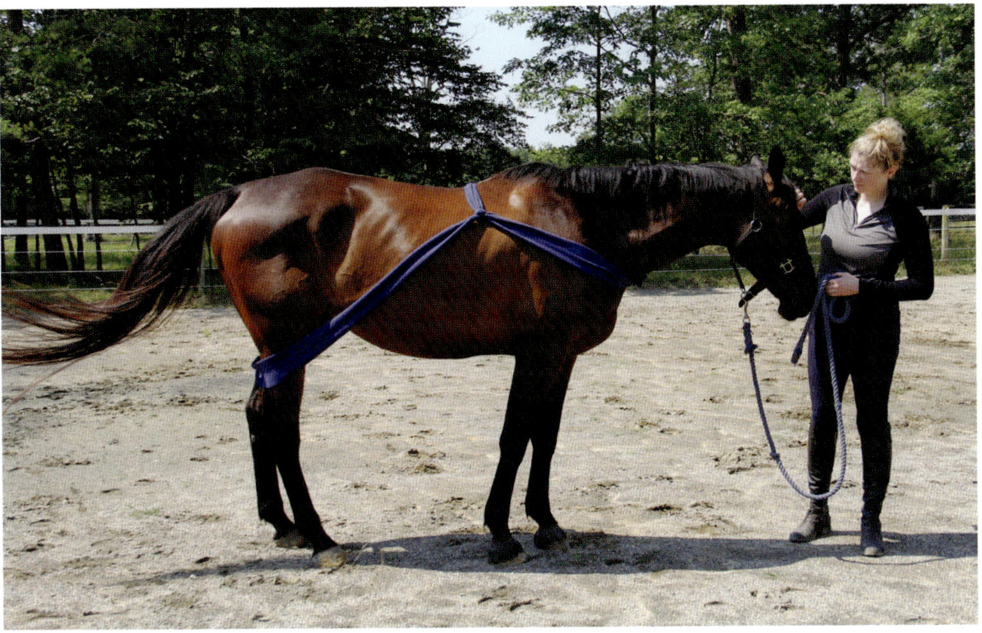

9.5 I use three polo wraps to create a sling around Mark's body. One is tied in a circle around his neck, and two are tied together to reach behind the hindquarters but above the hocks. As Mark moves, the wraps will act as a tactile, or physical, cue for him to engage both hind legs. He will not only be hyperaware of his separate limbs, but will also be encouraged to pull them underneath his body and away from the gentle resistance the slings create. The front band gives him awareness of his shoulders.

2 Wrap one bandage under the horse's neck and over or behind the withers. Tie securely.

3 The second wrap attaches to the first on either side of the withers and wraps around the hindquarters between the hip and the hock. These wraps should not be tight and restrictive, but should rest lightly—not loosely—on the body.

4 Leave the body wrap on and do in-hand work, longe, or even ride if the horse has become used to the wraps over several sessions (fig. 9.5).

Common Issues and Precautions

- Allow your horse time to get used to the feeling of the wraps and start work slowly. If the horse is nervous, you can start with just the neck wrap or just the hind wrap tied to a surcingle.

- Make sure the wraps can't slip or release and get caught under a foot or the horse's hocks.

Massage

tips for Massage

> A good body worker is worth the money every once in a while to help loosen your horse's hard-working muscles. Ask the therapist for tips to use yourself on a more regular basis.

WHAT

Massage stimulates the surface of the body. This increases blood flow and mechanically flushes the lymphatic system, which is responsible for fighting infection and metabolizing fluid. Joseph Pilates encouraged massage through "dry brushing" in order to cleanse the body, release toxins, and invigorate the skin.

WHY

- Broad massage strokes toward the heart help to activate the nervous system, relax tissue, decrease swelling, and increase lymphatic drainage.

- Massage relieves muscle restriction, frees adhesions and scar tissue, and improves range of motion.

- Improves blood and lymph circulation, enhances digestion, and strengthens the immune system.

HOW

1 Start with broad stokes down the neck and toward the kidneys, stroking toward the heart, liver, and excretory organs.

2 Next, use broad strokes up the leg to get blood flowing. Move on to "wringing" the legs, which involves the hands alternating in a wringing motion slowly up the leg toward the heart. Don't squeeze too hard, but just enough that skin is moving (fig. 9.6).

3 You can then begin pinching the skin of the lower-leg ligaments gently, pushing the skin up and down and moving in small sections up the leg. This will help move fluid up the limbs.

4 Finish with more broad strokes toward the kidneys to flush the toxins.

5 There are many different massage techniques you can use, but broad strokes are the easiest place to start. As mentioned previously, you can also use a lacrosse ball to deeply massage the muscles (see p. 172).

9.6 "Wringing" the legs is a massage technique that increases circulation in the limbs and helps break up sticky tissue. Gently squeeze the horse's leg in between your hands, and slowly move back and forth in a wringing motion up the leg, toward the heart.

Common Issues and Precautions

- Never massage directly on or below inflammation in the legs. The lymph system isolates injury with swelling to protect the body.

➤ Finding the right acupuncturist is essential. Make sure to ask for references.

➤ Sometimes acupuncture can be used as a diagnostic tool. When a horse becomes reactive to certain points, it may reveal specific pain or discomfort. While this can be helpful, it's important to not use acupuncture as a substitute for tradi-tional medicine.

WHAT

This modality uses needles to unblock the *chi/qi* or energy channels within the horse and restore balance in order to allow the horse to self-heal.

Different types of acupuncture are available including *dry needling* (more traditional), *aquapuncture* (injection of fluid), *electostimulation* (adding a pulsating electrical current), *moxibustion* (burning of an herb on acupuncture site), or simply using your hands to stimulate acu-puncture points.

WHY

- This alternative therapy is often used for arthritis, back pain, chronic pain, acute injuries, stress, muscle soreness, and general health and well-being.

- Increases circulation and relaxation.

HOW

1 Contact a certified veterinary acupuncturist.

2 You can use fingertip pressure at acupuncture points to help open the energy channels by yourself.

Common Issues and Precautions

- Acupuncture should only be used in conjunction with tradi-tional medicine, and not as a first response to serious ailments.

- Horses that are extremely anxious or aggressive and cannot remain still for treatment may not benefit from acupuncture.

- Multiple sessions could be needed to see a difference, and this can become costly.

Temperature Therapy

WHAT

As a general guide for using ice and heat, typically you should use ice for acute injuries and heat for chronic issues.

WHY

- Using the wrong temperature therapy can create more problems and elongate rehabilitation time.

- Cold reduces swelling and can produce numbing/pain relief, and heat can loosen tightness, relax the muscles, soothe pain, and help tissues become more elastic.

HOW

1 Icing can consist of cold hosing using the strongest setting so the body also gets massaged, ice boots, ice buckets, or even a liniment. Using 10 minutes for actual icing or 15–20 minutes for cold hosing is ideal. Icing for too long can signal the body to reopen blood vessels to protect the cold tissue, which can cause more damage.

2 Heating pads are useful for horses that are "cold-backed" or have a stiff back or pelvis. Make sure to have an extension cord handy and place a thin towel between your horse and the heating pad before resting it on the back, shoulders, or hind end for 10–15 minutes.

- It can be beneficial to ice the limbs after work when increasing intensity as a preventive tool.

- A good rule is to start with cold and use heat later. Heat should not be used on an acute injury for the first 24–48 hours.

- Heat permeates about 1½ inches while cold goes deeper and moist heat goes even deeper through the skin.

- Always put a layer of protection between your horse and a hot or cold compress.

- Gel packs can lose cooling ability quickly and start accumulating heat from the body.

- Wet towels or bandages placed in the freezer are a good option for DIY ice wraps, however, they can also lose cooling ability quickly.

- Don't use cold hosing on open wounds or nerve injuries.

- Do not put extremely cold water on a hot horse. If the horse is overheated, start with a sponge or spray between the front legs to bring his temperature down slowly.

- **Chiropractic:** A manual therapy that uses force to "adjust" and restore normal joint motion, stimulate nerve reflexes, and reduce pain. Often used to release a restriction within the joints or spine.

- **PEMF (Pulsed Electromagnetic Field) Therapy:** Said to relieve pain, decrease inflammation, increase circulation, reduce stiffness, activate the lymphatic system, stimulate acupuncture points, and improve general performance by stimulating cell metabolism.

- **Shockwave Therapy:** Specific application of energy or sound waves to reduce pain. Used most commonly on back pain, stress fractures, tendon injuries, navicular syndrome, and suspensory ligament injuries, it has even shown to help grow new blood vessels. While this modality stimulates and accelerates the healing process, it could also potentially damage healthy tissue. I have used it with success for back soreness.

- **Kinesiology Tape:** A special stretchy tape placed in specific areas on the horse to increase blood flow and pull skin in specific directions, allowing for decompression or support as needed. Much like a body wrap, it can improve range of motion or support the body from over-extending by increasing proprioception. If you have ever watched Olympic beach volleyball, kinesiology tape is what you see on the players' shoulders.

- **Acupressure Blankets:** Used by many yoga practitioners, acupressure can increase circulation, relax the connective tissue and sometimes calm a nervous horse. There are several blankets available commercially, as well as yoga mats that can be repurposed.

- **Light Therapy:** Stimulates cells that repair tissue, reduce inflammation, and relax the horse. This can be a beneficial tool for horses recovering from neurological issues. Equine-specific red light therapy pads include a combination of visible red LEDs and near-infrared LEDs.

Try to include bodywork 2–3 times a week and, if feasible, call a professional once a month.

How to Begin

Trust yourself. Pilates is an empowering method that all people can use for their own health and wellness, and to help strengthen their horse's mind and body as well. As a Pilates teacher, I often hear concerns that someone isn't flexible, or strong, or balanced enough to try Pilates. The reality is that this methodology can work for every body—all you have to do is have the courage to start.

Each exercise in this book can be useful for you whether you're a beginner or a professional, and whether you use a handful or all of them. Whatever your horse's current need, there is a modification to help better serve you. If you remember *why* you are doing each exercise, not just *how* to do it, you will be able to easily adjust or switch to a different exercise that hits the same muscle group in a different way, based on how your horse is feeling that day. Keep in mind the principles of Pilates as you work and ride:

- Control
- Center
- Concentration
- Precision
- Breath
- Flow
- Awareness
- Balance
- Efficiency
- Alignment
- Coordination
- Stamina
- Lengthening
- Harmony

Strive to find these principles in both yourself and your horse. Make goals and celebrate small milestones. Be safe, and have patience. Consult a vet when appropriate and find a trainer who is willing to work at your pace, setting a thoughtful and progressive training schedule for your horse. No matter your discipline, every exercise in this book can be utilized in some way to create a stronger, more mobile, and balanced horse. Above all, have fun!

After a year of dressage training and Pilates, Mark is slowly building correct and more balanced muscles (B). Your horse can, too!

Acknowledgments

Thank you to my mom, who drove me to the barn as a kid, bought my first horse, sat in the truck with me as I trailered to the vet for endless diagnostics, and continues to support my equine endeavors no matter how crazy or mundane—you're the absolute best. To my sister, Roberta, who not only took some of the photographs in this book, but also went with me to our first Pilates class. It was love at first teaser for both of us. To my dad, who worked hard so we could afford the trainers and horse shows. To my partner, Chris—my reluctant show groom, and the one who listens patiently to all my horse triumphs and woes. Thank you to Susan Mende, DVM, and Wolf Creek Equine, who diagnosed my horse's EPM after four other vets could not. You saved my horse's life. Thank you to my barn family, who support me, inspire me, and share their vast knowledge with me daily. Thank you to all the nutritionists, bodyworkers, and fitters I have gained knowledge from over the years. Finally, thank you to all the riders and trainers I've learned from, in person and from afar. Riders like Boyd Martin, Ingrid Klimke, Jim Wofford, Sharon White, Laine Ashker, and Redha Gharsa, who helped bring Mark back to work from our year of struggle and sickness—professionals that show us what good horsemanship looks like.

Index

Page numbers shown in *italics* indicate illustrations.